ROLE DRAMA

Carole Tarlington / Patrick Verriour

Acknowledgments

The authors wish to thank:

- the teachers and elementary students in Richmond and Vancouver who welcomed Carole into their classrooms to conduct the language sessions described in this book;
- the teachers attending in-service drama in education courses at the University of British Columbia;
- Linda Kaser, whose work in the BC Young Writers project helped make important connections between drama and writing;
- Vancouver Principal Malcolm Pratt for his encouragement;
- Margaret Burke for her suggestions; and
- Wendy Grant, without whose practical help this book could never have been written.

ROLE DRAMA

Carole Tarlington / Patrick Verriour

HEINEMANN
Portsmouth, NH

© 1991 Pembroke Publishers Limited
528 Hood Road
Markham, Ontario
L3R 3K9

Published in the U.S.A. by
Heinemann Educational Books, Inc.
361 Hanover Street
Portsmouth, NH 03801-3959
ISBN (U.S.) 0-435-08599-9

Canadian Cataloguing in Publication Data

Tarlington, Carole
  Role drama

Includes bibliographical references.
ISBN 0-921217-67-6

1. Drama in education. 2. Role playing.
I. Verriour, Patrick. II. Title.

PN3171.T37 1991   372.13'32   C91-094831-3

Library of Congress Cataloguing-in-Publication Data

Tarlington, Carole
  Role drama / Carole Tarlington, Patrick Verriour.
    p. cm.
  Includes bibliographical references.
  ISBN 0-435-08599-9
  1. Drama in education. I. Verriour, Patrick. II. Title.
PN3171.T37 1991   91-29266
372.13'32 -- dc20   CIP

Editor: Art Hughes
Designer: John Zehethofer
Cover Illustration: Pat Cupples
Typesetting: Jay Tee Graphics Ltd.

Printed and bound in Canada
9 8 7 6 5 4 3 2 1

Contents

Introduction

Drama! It's a strong word, one which contains a myriad of images and ideas for people, depending on their experiences. One of the difficulties in working with teachers and drama is tackling the confusion which exists around the word. In the past ten years we have given hundreds of workshops to teachers, administrators, and parents, and we often begin by doing a quick words association exercise with the word *drama*. The responses usually range from *theatre* words (lights, make-up, scenery, learning lines, improvisation, mime, movement, voice) through *self-expression* words (role-playing, creativity, free expression, cooperation) to *curriculum* words (language development, language registers, thinking, literature, playwriting) and, inevitably, *emotion* words (fun, terror, laughter, boredom).

Drama is all these things and more, and it is certainly beyond the scope of this book (indeed, beyond us!) to deal with *all* that drama is. This book focuses on *role drama*. In it, we offer practical advice to teachers who want to use role drama as a teaching strategy in their classrooms. The role dramas described here spring from various sources — literature, social studies, family life, and environmental issues. We would like to emphasize that the role dramas described in chapters 3, 4, and 5 are descriptions of lessons that have actually occurred in classrooms; they are not intended as model lesson plans.

Drama for thinking, drama for feeling, and drama for reflection are all important elements of the role dramas described in this book. In the hands of a skillful and sensitive teacher, role drama can be a powerful mode of learning across the school curriculum. In the medium of role drama, students are encouraged to work cooperatively, to question assumptions, exchange ideas, solve problems, and share their own personal knowledge.

Above all, role drama places students in a position to identify with different fields of human endeavor at a personal level. It encourages them to look beyond the obvious and to create meaning for themselves rather than just accepting the teacher's interpretation of a learning experience. Comparing the role of the teacher in the classroom to that of the child's care giver in the home, Courtnay Cazden (1988) writes that education is primarily concerned with teaching students to see phenomena in new ways, "to reconceptualize circles as wheels or wheels as circles" (*Classroom Discourse*, 112). According to Cazden, this process of "reconceptualization" is best achieved when children are placed in learning contexts which have purpose and meaning so that when they are presented with alternative meanings, these do not deny the validity of the personal beliefs, understandings, and values they bring with them to school.

1
....

What is role drama?

Role drama is a *powerful method of teaching* that aims at promoting a change of understanding or insight for the participants.

It is like walking in someone else's shoes — exploring the thoughts and feelings of another person by responding and behaving as that person would in a given situation.

In role drama, teachers set up imagined situations which students and teachers enter together, *in role*, to explore events, issues, and relationships. What distinguishes role drama from other kinds of drama is that *the teacher takes a role within the drama.*

Its purposes are to help the participants
- examine the perceptions and points of view of others
- integrate language, feeling, and thought
- develop skills in problem-solving and decision-making
- enlarge experience
- research, read, and write about topics connected with the drama.

Since role drama enables people to grapple with thought and language in a meaningful context, it is an important strategy for promoting independent thinking, cooperative learning, and whole language.

Basic principles

1. *The process is cognitive.* A popular misconception is that drama

activities are done to make the participants 'feel good'. Drama is often seen as purely expressive; the cognitive demands are totally ignored. In fact, students involved in role drama are engaged in thoughtful work which requires that they enter the discipline of the art form of theatre, where they work as actors, directors, playwrights, and audience.

During role drama, students:

- face issues
- examine attitudes
- grasp concepts
- solve problems
- research
- observe
- make judgments
- reflect
- extend language
- make and test hypotheses
- draw conclusions
- talk and write in a variety of styles
- concentrate
- cooperate with others
- learn content of the subject
- gain self-confidence
- analyze situations and characters
- defend a point of view
- make inferences
- listen critically
- translate ideas from verbal to visual and vice versa.

Thus, during role drama, participants are consistently working at the higher levels of Bloom's taxonomy (N.A.D.I.E. Papers 1, 1984).

2. *The process involves a group.* Role drama is a group learning experience requiring a high degree of cooperation. During their time together, the members of the group learn to work cooperatively to solve problems. Thus, through role drama, it is possible to realize the potential of group decision-making.

3. *The process is collaborative.* During role drama, the power is shared with the students, who take responsibility for their actions. This sharing enables young people and adults to work together as collaborators. Working collaboratively involves a shift in the teacher's role from one who is dominating the curriculum to one who is opening up possibilities for exploration and interpretation. The teacher is no longer the centre of power in the classroom but rather an adult collaborator and guide. Often in role drama, the teacher deliberately takes on the role of one who needs help, thus shifting the power base to the students.

4. *The process requires the teacher to take on a role within the drama.* The teacher in role is a unique teaching strategy which enables the teacher to challenge the student's thinking from within the drama. In role, the teacher can challenge, arouse, create tension, open possibilities, support the group, or play devil's advocate. The teacher in role approach does not require that the teacher be a skilled actor; rather it requires that the teacher be willing to stand in someone else's shoes for a short time, reflecting a different stance or set of attitudes for the group to deal with.

5. *The process requires skilled questioning.* The kind of thinking done by the group is very much influenced by the kinds of questions posed. The secret of skilled questioning lies in asking 'real' questions as opposed to 'teacher-type' questions, that is, questions to which the teacher already knows the answers.

Schools, it seems, are the only places where people ask questions to which they already know the answers. Normally, people employ questions when they need information. (Outside a classroom, I wouldn't ask you what time it was if I already knew. In fact, it would be quite rude of me to do so!) Using questions in this teacher-type way trains young people to think that questions are used to test what you already know rather than to seek knowledge. It also leads them to believe that someone, somewhere has the answer to everything. Why should they take time to think of an answer? The notion that we need to grapple with questions and make our own decisions about many things is often foreign to young people. This is a dangerous by-product of the way questioning is used in schools.

6. *The process requires teachers to slow down.* Complex thinking requires time. Teachers must be prepared to wait for students to think things through. Young teachers in training used to be taught to 'keep up the pace of the lesson,' asking questions in rapid fire and waiting only one second for an answer. Obviously this is a good strategy if you want students to know things by rote, but if you want them to think deeply then you must allow time for reflection. This means you must slow down and be prepared to wait for answers. One of the hardest things about this approach is the waiting, in silence, as students think things through, but it's always worth the waiting.

Role drama across the curriculum

Because role drama is a teaching method and not a subject, it can be used in different areas of the curriculum. If you want your students to learn multiplication tables, role drama is probably not the method you would employ. However, if the curriculum is centred around inquiry, role drama can be used successfully. Since role drama frequently focuses on issues and understandings, it is particularly effective in social studies, literature, language arts, and science.

Role drama and language learning

Teachers who have used role drama as a learning strategy know instinctively that they are always working with a whole language approach. In role drama, students speak, write, read, listen, and present their ideas verbally and visually within contexts that have purpose and meaning for them. Literature is frequently used as a source, so that students work with all aspects of language in an integrated, meaningful manner.

Perhaps the most positive aspect of role drama is that students are compelled to use language in a variety of ways. Sometimes a letter must be written or a report compiled, and the students, in role, tackle these language tasks energetically as they know that completing them will help make the drama work. The drama thus becomes a strong motivating force for language work.

Whole language is a child-centred, literature-based approach to language and teaching that immerses students in real communication situations wherever possible (Froese 1990, 1). The whole language teacher believes that language is a naturally developing human activity which should not be separated into 'subjects' to be taught, such as composition, reading, and spelling. Instead, language is learned for the purpose of communication and used holistically before being refined and differentiated. Froese says that the classroom can create a context for 'real life' language situations so that collaborative learning, critical thinking, and creativity are encouraged. In whole language classrooms, student interest should drive much of the daily learning so that students are encouraged to develop a sense of ownership in the learning "through working with their ideas" (Froese 1990, 8).

Most whole language programs are designed so that students

are encouraged to plan their own learning activities. Many teachers therefore create learning centres, such as reading or writing, where students may work independently, with partners, and in groups. Throughout this book, emphasis is placed on a group, collaborative approach to role drama, demonstrating how, with a little imagination and planning, role drama can be taught to the whole class or to small groups working by themselves.

Sources for role drama

Sources for role drama are as varied as the subjects in the students' curriculum and the interests and issues these generate.

• *Stories told, read, or heard.* To be effective for role drama, stories must have an interesting issue that is worth exploring, a group or groups of people who are involved in the issue, and possibilities for tension and surprise.

• *Issues from social studies.* Social studies curricula are issue-based and therefore present many opportunities for role drama. For example, putting students into role as both native people and government representatives will help them gain a deeper understanding of the complexities of land treaties.

• *Poetry.* The poem should reflect a feeling or idea that would appeal to the age level and maturity of the group. Younger students might enjoy working with nursery rhymes. For example, in the "Queen of Hearts," the Knave of Hearts stole some tarts. "What caused him to steal?" and "How does a community deal with thieving?" are two issues that arise out of this seemingly simple rhyme. Older students might prefer the social issue expressed in E.A. Robinson's poem "Richard Cory" and the Paul Simon song of the same title (Why should a rich young man with apparently everything choose to take his own life?) or the environmental issue expressed in Pete Seeger's song "Pollution."

• *A picture or photograph.* A famous painting or current newspaper photograph could be used to create a sense of place, time, or character. A photo of newly arrived immigrants or a picture of an industrial site showing pollution may inspire a dramatic response.

• *A piece of writing.* Using parts of a document, such as an ancient manuscript or an old letter, can create mystery. This kind of situation has a degree of authenticity since old documents do not often survive intact.

• *A map.* This can be created by the students or the teacher or it can be a real map, depending on what kind of drama is being done. For instance, a pirate drama may involve presenting a teacher-made map to the group, or the teacher may ask students, in role as pirates, to draw a map so they can return later for their treasure. As a starting point for another drama, the teacher, in role as an explorer, may present to fellow explorers a real map of the terrain to be crossed.

• *A snatch of taped conversation.* A message left on an answering machine can be used by the teacher, in role as a detective, as the last contact from a missing invididual, or teacher and class, in role as espionage agents, can attempt to crack a coded message left by a missing colleague.

• *A closed box.* This is an effective device for creating mystery and tension. For instance, students, in role as archaeologists, find a sealed box which has not been opened for centuries, a box which bears a warning as in the case of Pandora's box.

• *A museum display.* Personal belongings of a fur trader or war veteran, children's toys of another era or country, ancient coins or artifacts may inspire dramatic response.

• *A piece of jewellery.* The teacher, in role as a police inspector, may say to the class, in role as detectives: "This is the only piece of jewellery left behind in the robbery. It was not overlooked but left behind deliberately. Why?"

• *A piece of clothing.* The teacher and class are in role as documentary film-makers. The teacher holds up a black leather jacket bearing strange designs. "The members of the gang who are terrorizing this elementary school wear these jackets. Does anyone know the significance of these markings?"

• *A paragraph from an historical document.* Significant paragraphs from documents, such as Native Indian treaties or land claims or the U.N. Declaration of Children's and/or Women's Rights, may be used to stimulate response.

• *A diary entry.* An imaginary diary entry written by a character in a book or a person in history may serve as a source. An entry from a student or teacher journal would serve as well.

• *A letter.* Letters may include one from Santa to his elves informing them he's going out of the toy business and that they are going to be laid off; or a collective letter from the students to the school board challenging a board decision. For an example of how a letter can be used in role drama, see the section on "The Pied Piper."

• *Reports by psychologist, police officer, school principal, etc.* Various reports may be used to trigger role play: report of a psychologist's interview with a teen gang member, written by either the teacher or students after interviewing students, in role as teen gang members; psychologists' reports of interviews with nursery rhyme characters, such as Humpty Dumpty, the Knave of Hearts, or the old woman who lived in a shoe; police officer's report of an accident or crime; business manager's report of a crisis that has to be settled.

• *Secret documents.* Special documents, invented by the teacher or students, could give details of environmental, military, or community problems that have not yet been made public. The class could be in role as reporters, government officials, or concerned citizens.

Using folktales for role drama

Several years ago we worked with a group of bright, middle-class Grade 5 and 6 children in an affluent area of Vancouver. They were delightful, intelligent, sensitive, thoughtful, artistic young people. We decided to do role drama around the themes that occur in "The Pied Piper." The issue of broken contracts and revenge seemed natural for this kind of work. We had not intended to tell the group the story, assuming that they would be familiar with this classic tale since they were a well read group.

To our astonishment, we discovered that only one of the students really knew the story. Most had heard of it or had some shreds of knowledge, but on the whole it was unknown. We were both surprised and dismayed. How would these young people fare when they entered secondary school and began studying literature?

Through early exposure to folktales, young people gain a basic understanding of good and evil in story, and this helps them later to understand the concept of protagonist and antagonist in literature. These tales also contain universal themes which occur again and again not only in our literature but, more importantly, in the literature of different cultures. The story of Cinderella, for instance, appears in many cultures — Asian, European, and Nordic and, according to Jane Yolen (*Favorite Folktales from around the World*, 1986), has over 500 versions and has been told and handed down for centuries.

Folktales have survived through hundreds of years because their themes are universal and the issues and dilemmas they address are classic. Their themes reappear in TV dramas, such as "Dallas" and "The Young and the Restless," in film and TV westerns, and in Shakespeare's plays! Love, treachery, broken promises, evil and good fighting for supremacy — these themes have intrigued and entertained audiences since time began. Knowing these stories is a very important part of children's education. In *The Uses of Enchantment*, prominent psychologist Bruno Bettleheim argues that folktales are necessary for children's emotional and personal development. Our teaching experience has borne this out.

From that experience we decided to devote a fair proportion of our work to using folktales as a source for role drama. We also discovered that for teachers, using folktales is a reassuring and concrete way to start, much easier than simply beginning with the question, "What would you like your play to be about today?"

Telling rather than reading stories to children

In our extensive and varied teaching careers, we have worked with many students with reading problems. Those students who have trouble comprehending do not seem to have any 'pictures in their heads' when they read. For example, after reading about a young man asleep in his room in a simple cottage in the woods, some students cannot describe the cottage. In fact, if asked, they are baffled by the question, scanning the passage and saying, "It doesn't say." For these children the whole process of reading is different from what it is for us. From our own experience and from working with fluent readers, we know that we have a kind of 'movie' running through our heads when we read and, if asked to supply details, we can do so readily because we have been conjuring images all along. We realized therefore that any help in image making that could be given to 'poor readers' would be a positive step. Storytelling is one such step.

When telling a story, the storyteller and the audience are in direct contact. No book separates them. The storyteller creates images with words and the listeners make their own images to go with these words. This is an active process and, although everyone may be sitting still, the audience is actively involved with the story.

When reading a story, the teacher usually holds the book so that the students can see the illustrations. In current editions of folktales, these illustrations are often wonderful, fully colored, and beautiful. So, when the teacher reads, "Once upon a time there was a leafy green forest. . .," the students are presented immediately with a beautiful, detailed illustration of the forest scene. The problem, however, is that the image, no matter how wonderful, has been prepared for them so that viewing illustrations can become a passive activity, like television, with the students simply receiving others' images instead of making their own. This is not to suggest that students should *never* view others' images. It is important for their appreciation of art and design that they do. What we are advocating is that teachers learn to *tell* stories as well as read them, and make a practice of telling at least 50 percent of the stories to their classes.

"Oh, no!" many teachers cry. "I can't do that! I can't tell stories. You are just a natural storyteller. It is easy for you, but I can't." Of course this is not so. It may be relatively easy for experienced storytellers but they, too, had to make a beginning. The first time you tell a class a story you may be nervous and the telling may not be brilliant, but children are very forgiving and they will put up with you while you get to be expert. It isn't easy, but every teacher can become a storyteller.

We offer the following tips for the beginning storyteller:

- Read the story you have decided to tell as many times as you can bear. In order to retell it, you must know it.
- If you are nervous, make a list of what happens in the story. For example, in "Jack Simpson," the Miller and his beautiful daughter

live in a simple cottage; the King goes riding and stops at their cottage; the Miller tells the King that his daughter can spin straw into gold; the King invites them to the Palace . . . and so on.

- Tell the story to someone or something, such as your toddler, partner, cat, or tape machine.
- Tell it again. Practise putting as much life into it as possible. Experiment with different voices and gestures for various characters in the story.
- Practise and play with it again and again, never underestimating the power of rehearsal. By rehearsing the story you make it your own, stamping it with your unique way of telling. Rehearse it until you feel good about it.
- Tell it to your class. If you have never done this before and you are nervous about it, tell them. Ask them to help you out by criticizing what you've done. They will. And they will be generous. You are guaranteed to enjoy it tremendously. Many teachers, convinced that they cannot tell a story, finally do it, and do it well. They come to us with shining eyes, full of stories of how wonderful it was and how their classes responded so well and how much they all enjoyed it.

Storytelling is a joy for both teller and audience. Don't miss out on it.

Frequently asked questions about role drama

Q. *What about discipline? When you put yourself in the role of someone who needs help, aren't you giving up control? You aren't in control any longer. I can see real problems with that.*
A. Often in role drama, you put yourself in a role where the children know more than you do and this means they have more power. However, the great advantage of role drama is that you are still in the drama, and from your position within it you can ask questions which lead children to consider the implications of their actions. You are also able to play devil's advocate, or introduce another point of view which the group may not, on its own, consider. One of the principles of this way of working is sharing power with the students. In role drama, when young people are handed power, they are handed the responsibility to make decisions, consider consequences, and care about moral dilemmas common to human beings. Power and responsibility

go hand in hand. If we expect young people to take decision-making seriously, we must take seriously their right to make decisions.

Q. *What do you do with the children who don't want to take part?*
A. There are no special discipline rules for drama. Do the same as you would do with the child who refuses to do math. One of the good things about drama, though, is that you do have some built in help.

At the beginning of the drama you can make a contract with the children. "I will agree to do this, if you agree to that. Does that interest you?" When you make such a contract, make eye contact with the children, and check that they are agreeing to go along with the drama. If you see that someone is reluctant, say, "I know what I am asking isn't all that easy, but I will help you to do this, if you will agree to try. Is it agreed?" Usually the child will agree, having the additional security of knowing that you will help.

If anyone does not do what's asked, remind that student of the contract, simply saying, "I thought we agreed to this? Didn't we?" The child will usually cooperate. If this still doesn't work, and the child is destroying the drama, you should do whatever you do generally with children who disrupt the class's work. The main thing is to let the children know that you are serious about this kind of work and you expect them to be serious about it too. Drama work is just as important and serious as mathematics. Expect that they will do it and do it well.

Q. *In my classroom I have quite a few children who aren't proficient in English. What would you do about them in this work?*
A. Because language is learned in context, make no special arrangements for these children during the drama. This work creates a meaningful context for their use of language. We have seen children whose English is minimal, so caught up in the emotion of trying to convince the Piper to return the children that they struggle to find the language to convince him. They are so involved in the drama that they lose their self-consciousness about saying it 'right' simply to make themselves understood. Often role drama brings to the surface the child's passive knowledge of language and makes it active. Of course, if most of your students do not have enough English to even understand the story,

you should illustrate with pictures and take whatever steps you would normally take to ensure that they understand what is happening in the story.

Q. *Can I use the stories in my reader to do this work?*
A. Of course, providing that the particular story has two essential elements:

(1) *A compelling issue* that you can formulate into a key question.

(2) *A group entry.* All of your students should be able to enter the drama together. If you act out "The Story of Jack Simpson", there are three or four key roles, and everyone else in the class 'carries a spear'. However, the invention of roles of the Advisors makes it possible for all of the students to enter the role drama in important roles. "The Pied Piper", on the other hand, has lots of group entries. There is a group of children, a group of townspeople, a group of councillors, and there could be groups of rat-trap makers and designers.

Q. *How do I find other stories suitable for role drama?*
A. Some are offered in this book and some are suggested in the books listed in the bibliography, especially Cecily O'Neill's *Drama Guidelines* and Geoff Davies' *Practical Primary Drama*. Many folktales are suitable. When you are trying to judge whether the story is suitable, look for stories with compelling issues which you think people of all ages would find interesting to tackle, and look within the stories for groups of people with problems. Dorothy Heathcote once said that drama was about "man in a mess". It is. Look for those stories about people in trouble. If they are a group, that's great. If they aren't a group, you will have to invent a group which could be involved. In one drama workshop Juliana Saxton read "Cinderella" to us, closed the book and said, "Well, as if it wasn't bad enough having that huge ball to organize, we've now got this wedding to plan. Are the cooks all here?"

A group entry was created. The teachers in the workshop became the behind-the-scene organizers of the royal wedding. Cooks created menus, organized food lists, sorted out catering problems, and generally became responsible for this important event. It was a perfect example of devising a group entry from a story about individuals.

Q. *Is it a good idea to use costumes and/or props?*

A. Both can be useful. A word of caution, however. Make sure that the piece of costume and/or prop assists the drama and does not distract from it.

We once observed a drama where a cardboard crown was used. It kept falling off the King's head and the drama became focused around how to keep it on and whether it was going to fall off again. In this case, it would have been better to get rid of it. The children knew this and would have been very happy had the teacher simply said, "Do you think this crown is necessary? Can we believe he is King without it?" The children could and would have been happy to dispose of it. Unfortunately, this did not happen and the crown ruined the drama.

In another situation, a teacher decided to go into role as the Mayor. She left the room to prepare for the role while the children organized themselves into a meeting. They were rat-trap designers, and they were going to present their designs to the Mayor.

When the teacher returned, she carried a large hammer, which she placed on the desk before her. Generally, the meeting went well, but observers could see that the children were constantly aware of the hammer. At the finish of the drama, the first question asked was "Why did the Mayor carry that hammer?"

The teacher replied, "Oh, that wasn't a hammer. It was a gavel! I was going to use it to call the meeting to order if it got noisy.

For the children, however, it was a hammer, and many of them spent all their time wondering about it, and not about the issues the teacher wanted them to focus on. She could have avoided this by simply telling them before the drama, "Did you know that often meetings are kept in order by the use of a gavel? A gavel looks something like a hammer but is usually made of wood. The person with the gavel is the chairperson, and the gavel is a symbol of power. As we don't have a gavel, I thought we could use this hammer instead. Would that be all right, do you think?

Of course the children would have agreed. They do this all the time in their own play, and they could then have focused on the important issues. They would also have learned something about symbols, and perhaps a new word as well.

Q. *I'm amazed at how structured your lesson actually was. Is structure a key issue in this type of lesson?*

A. Structure is a key issue in any lesson. Careful planning is necessary if teachers want their children to learn. It is the teacher's job to structure class time so the children learn.

Q. *What if you get stumped and can't think of what to do next?*
A. The great strength of role drama is you can simply stop anytime, and all the better if it is at a tense moment. You simply go out of role and you can do one of two things:

(1) Say, "Well, that Queen was really stumped. And I must admit, so am I. Has anyone any suggestions as to what could happen next?" The children will have ideas. All you have to do is act on one of their suggestions.

(2) Say, "Well, that's where we'll stop for today. We'll pick this up tomorrow. Take out your math books." This gives you time to do some more thinking and planning before the next lesson. Don't worry that the children won't remember where they are the next day. This way of working is vivid to children. They will remember where they left off and be happy to go on with the drama, providing the interest is there. If it isn't, then you should shelve it anyway, and do something else which does interest, challenge and stimulate them.

Q. *You took a great deal of time establishing a 'mind set' for your students. Is this always necessary? Can you work more quickly?*
A. Time spent building belief and commitment is always time well spent. Students who have thought, interviewed, written, and done still imaging become more deeply involved with the work and will think more deeply as they are drawn more deeply into it. One of the basic principles of this type of drama work is that you move slowly, allowing time for reflection and higher-order thinking. However, as children become more experienced working this way, they can move more quickly into the drama, needing less time to build belief and commitment.

Q. *I realize that questioning is important. You seem to have an endless supply of questions in your head. How can I learn to ask the sort of questions which will help my students think within the drama?*
A. In *Teaching Drama*, Norah Morgan and Juliana Saxton have written an excellent chapter on questioning. This is a good place to begin.

Also remember to listen with all of yourself to the children in role, and ask questions because *you* want the answers, not because you want to test whether they can come up with the answer which you already have in your mind.

Q. *Do you have to be an actor to work this way?*
A. No. However, you do have to be prepared to try and think like someone else rather than like a teacher. It is amusing to hear teachers say that they can't do this, because every day teachers adopt a variety of roles, in classrooms and in life, without any trouble at all. All people do. The person you are at home with your family is probably different from the teacher who talks with parents, and different again from the person who plays devil's advocate in class or in the staff room just to see how people will cope with the other side of an argument. To put yourself into another person's shoes is a learning experience, for you as well as for your students.

Q. *How do you evaluate this work?*
A. Evaluate through the products which come out of the role drama — the writing, the art work, and the quality of oral discussion. This way of working is not suggested as a subject but rather as a method of teaching that creates a thinking environment in your classroom. It seems sensible, therefore, to evaluate the products of the thinking. Try, however, not to make the mistake of thinking that because a student is not talking, s/he is not thinking. Participation does not always mean talking. Participation also means thinking, and that's why it is sensible to evaluate the products which come out of the drama. A student who has not said anything in a drama will often write very thoughtfully, proving that silence does not equal lack of participation.

Selected references

Barton, Bob and David Booth. *Stories in the Classroom: Storytelling, Reading Aloud, and Roleplaying with Children.* Markham, Ontario: Pembroke Publishers Limited/ Portsmouth, New Hampshire: Heinemann Educational Books, 1990.

Bettleheim, Bruno. *The Uses of Enchantment.* New York: Vintage Books, 1977.

Froese, Victor, ed. *Whole-Language: Practice and Theory.* Toronto: Prentice Hall, 1990.

Schafner, Megan, et al. *Drama, Language and Learning.* Hobart: N.A.D.I.E. Papers. National Association of Drama in Education, 1984.

2

....

Planning your own role dramas

This chapter describes ways to plan role dramas that enable students to 'reconceptualize' their present understandings by taking fresh perspectives and by working in contexts that involve human problems with which they can personally identify. To begin, here are steps to plan a role drama using "The Pied Piper" as a source.

Planning a role drama based on "The Pied Piper"

Careful planning is necessary if a role drama is to work. The steps outlined by Ken Byron in his article "Indians and Pioneers" in *2D Journal*, 1985 are adapted and reproduced here. If you work through these planning steps, your role drama is guaranteed to work.

Following are the planning steps involved in using "The Pied Piper" as a source for drama.

BEGIN BY CHOOSING YOUR TOPIC

In this case, the topic is "The Pied Piper," a story that has a number of potential learning areas.

SEGMENT THE TOPIC AND IDENTIFY THE LEARNING AREAS

Identify the learning areas within the topic that you may wish to pursue with your students. It is worthwhile to spend considerable time here, because investigating the topic opens it up, produces many ideas, and helps later when you are looking for enrichment areas to explore with your students.

The following web shows some of the possibilities opened up by this story. There are more. This is not a definitive list but a peek at one teacher's thinking.

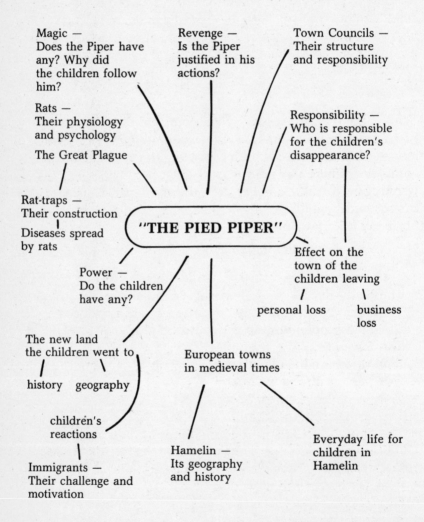

SELECT THE LEARNING AREA AND FORMULATE A KEY QUESTION

It is important to choose a clear focus to begin with, even though new foci may appear as the drama unfolds. Once you have chosen the learning area you wish to pursue, formulate a *key question* from that learning area. In order for this question to work for role drama, it must have human conflict within it. For example, the question, "What was the new land like that the children went to?" is not as suitable as "How did the children react to the new land they were taken to?" or "How did the Pied Piper cope with the children once they arrived in the new land?" Each of the second questions introduces human conflict and centres around individuals. Each is personal and has the potential for tension and surprise, two important elements of drama.

LIST THE POSSIBLE VIEWPOINTS AND DEFINE CONTEXTS

Identify the viewpoints that the class and teacher could adopt in order to become involved in the key question. Obviously the viewpoint affects how the key question looks. Again, spend time thinking here. Make a list of all the possible viewpoints, taking care to go beyond the most obvious. Making such a list can open up many new possibilities.

POSSIBLE VIEWPOINTS IN "THE PIED PIPER"

- The children
- The Pied Piper
- The Pied Piper's family
- The townspeople of Hamelin
- The Mayor and Councillors of Hamelin
- The ruler of the new land
- The people in the new land
- The army in the new land
- The church officials in the new land
- Historians
- The chamber of commerce in the new land
- Pediatricians in the new land
- Film crew
- Museum curators
- School psychologists in the new land

Place each viewpoint within a context. The context must be presented in such a way that those within it are faced with a problem which needs resolving. For example:

VIEWPOINTS	POSSIBLE CONTEXTS
The children	• In Hamelin before the Pied Piper came into their lives. • At a brief meeting in the new land where they are being told what arrangements are being made for them. • At a meeting where they are trying to decide whether they want to go home or not.
The Pied Piper	• Meeting with members of the community to explain why he brought the children to the new land and to ask for families to adopt them. • Meeting with the children to explain why they have been brought there. • Meeting with the children to listen to their complaints about the new land.
The Pied Piper's family	• Meeting to discuss what can be done about the Pied Piper's temper and subsequent rash behavior.
The Mayor and Council	• At a council meeting after the children have disappeared, deciding what is to be done.
The ruler of the new land	• Meeting with a group from the community who want the children sent away as they are causing a strain on the town's resources.
The army in the new land	• Meeting to work out the logistics of housing and feeding this group of children who have arrived in the town as refugees.
Church officials	• Meeting to look at the ethical and moral implications of the children's arrival.
Historians	• In the 1990s commissioned by the ancestors of the children of Hamelin to write an accurate account of the event for school texts.

Chamber of commerce	• Meeting to discuss the effect of all these new people on business in the new land.
School officials in the new land	• Meeting to discuss how they can handle the crisis in the schools caused by the arrival of so many new children.
Pediatricians in the new land	• Meeting to discuss how they can handle the crisis caused by the arrival of so many new potential patients.
Film crew	• Meeting to decide on the key incidents of the events in order to produce a TV documentary entitled *Where Have All the Children Gone?*

CHOOSE A CONTEXT FOR THE DRAMA AND ROLES FOR YOURSELF AND STUDENTS

All of the above contexts demand some sort of action to be taken. All that is needed is for you to choose *ONE* of these contexts to begin with. Once you have selected a context, choose a viewpoint (role) for yourself and one for the students. Remember that the best roles are those which create tension. If, for instance, you choose "Pediatricians in the new land" as a viewpoint for both yourself and your students, it may be better if you take on the role of the pediatrician who is of the opinion that these young people are not your responsibility and they should be sent elsewhere, rather than just the head pediatrician of the hospital who asks, "What are we going to do?"

When you examine your list, you may get some new ideas for a context. For example, if you take on the role of an army major, the children may be in role as school board officials. You come to their meeting because you think it is unfair that the army be given the sole responsibility of organizing the children. You want the school officials to help in some way, perhaps with money or personnel.

ACTIVITIES FOR BUILDING BELIEF AND COMMITMENT

Engage the children through activities that foster belief and commitment in the drama. Those might include storytelling, narration, drawing, writing, guided imagery, making lists, interviewing, still image, making maps or plans, questioning, or thinking.

SET UP THE ROOM PHYSICALLY

To help create the context for the students, prepare the room for drama. This can be simply rearranging desks to a meeting format or it can involve quite complicated changes including lighting and furniture. This is entirely up to you. However, a good rule of thumb is not to have things in your drama area which do not belong, such as pencil cases and stuffed toys, or walkmans. In the theatre, only those things which have meaning for the play are on set. It should be the same in role drama.

WRITE A SCRIPT FOR YOURSELF IN ROLE

This script is the one you will use when you first go into role. Plan it carefully so that it gives all the information necessary, and make sure it speaks with the voice of the role you are trying to create. Ask yourself, "Does this sound like the head pediatrician, or does it just sound like a teacher pretending?" Often we are so conditioned to speaking to children with our 'teacher' voice, that it is difficult to adopt another role. Writing your script enables you to look at your character carefully before you go into role. When you enter in role, the children should immediately grasp who they are, where they are, and what is happening. Rehearse your script so that you signal these things clearly to your students.

INJECT THE DRAMA WITH TENSION

This is what drives the drama, keeping everyone interested. Some kinds of tension are:

- Tension of secrecy. "I'm glad none of you mentioned this meeting to the Pied Piper. I wanted us all to feel free to say what's on our minds without feeling intimidated."
- Tension of mystery. "I'm not sure just where he got this latest group of children, are you?"
- Tension of an obstacle to be overcome. "We have to solve this problem of where to put the children or there is going to be real trouble in this community."

- Tension of time — of waiting — or sense of urgency. "He's been in there for a long time talking to those children. The people outside are getting restless."
- Tension of space and distance.
- Tension of a dare, challenge, or test.
- Tension of depending on one another.
- Tension of conflicting priorities.
- Tension of status.

For a full description of tension and how it can be used, see *Teaching Drama: A Mind of Many Wonders,* by Norah Morgan and Juliana Saxton.

If you use all of the above steps in your planning, you can't go wrong. Remember, though, that *all* of these steps are necessary. Don't skip any. This way of planning will work for any kind of drama, whether it springs from a literature source, an issue from social studies, or a topic suggested by the class. Recently, a student teacher expressed amazement at the planning required for role drama. "I thought it was so much more spontaneous!" he said. Careful planning, of course, is at the heart of all good teaching. Once a plan has been made, it is possible to deviate from it, depending on how the group responds or what it suggests. However, the teacher should have a clear idea of what the role drama is going to explore and must have a clear focus for the lesson.

Role dramas based on social studies topics

The following role drama plans are based on social studies topics. Each plan is similar to that of "The Pied Piper", and each one includes several activities for building belief.

The first drama, about a Circus Community, would be suitable for Grades 3 through 5, while the second, a Mining Community, could be taught to Grades 4 through 6. The final drama, the Effects of a Nuclear Disaster, is intended for Grades 7, 8, and 9. Please remember that these are suggested grade levels. You may find your class is ready to tackle a drama recommended for another grade level. For example, with some adaptations and modifications, the Circus Community drama could be used with Grades 1 or 2, and the Nuclear Disaster drama with Grade 6. Some adaptation activities are included in the outlines.

Planning a role drama for the circus community

TOPIC

A circus community.

SEGMENT THE TOPIC AND IDENTIFY THE LEARNING AREAS

- Protection and preservation of animal life. The ethics of keeping animals in captivity and training them to perform tricks that are not natural to them.
- The hazards and dangers of circus performance acts. Which is considered of first importance, the safety of the performers or the entertainment of the audience?
- The impact of the circus on a small town community. Social, environmental, and financial outcomes.
- The circus community. Is it a tightly-knit family, a hierarchical business organization, or something else?
- Tradition versus change. Updating circus acts and other attractions to remain competitive in the 1990s and beyond.
- The history and origins of the traveling circus. Problems associated with running a circus. Recruiting circus acts, coping with seasonal changes, dealing with accidents, animal rights activists, balancing the books.

SELECT THE LEARNING AREA AND FORMULATE A KEY QUESTION

Is life in the circus as glamorous as it is sometimes made out to be?

LIST POSSIBLE VIEWPOINTS AND DEFINE CONTEXTS

VIEWPOINT	POSSIBLE CONTEXTS
The circus entertainers/trainers	• At winter headquarters, rehearsing for the season: new arrivals at the circus meet other members of the troupe faced with lay-offs — who will have to go?
Visitors to the circus	• Waiting for the circus to come and, at the end, saying goodbye.

32

Neighborhood residents	• Complaining to city council about the noise and garbage.
Talent scouts	• Looking for new acts.
Publicity manager	• Arranging a circus parade, making advertisements, and meeting the press to answer charges of animal ill treatment.
Film crew	• Making a film documentary about circus life.
Circus manager	• Seeking help to keep the circus on the road and deal with animal activist groups.

CHOOSE A CONTEXT FOR THE DRAMA AND ROLES FOR YOURSELF
AND STUDENTS

To choose a focus that will enable you and your students to explore the key question, "Is life in the circus as glamorous as it is sometimes made out to be?", choose a viewpoint and context that will give the class an opportunity to experience the thrills, excitements, and disappointments of being a circus performer.

For example, if you choose "Entertainers/trainees rehearsing for the season," the students could take on the roles of trainee circus performers. After brainstorming with the students the different sorts of acts that might be seen at a circus, such as juggling, clowning, or high-wire walking, students should work in pairs to prepare their acts, working in mime.

After taking time to discuss their performance acts, younger students show a great deal of ingenuity in their presentations. Working in mime means that they have to plan their acts step by step so that they finally have a polished short performance. Some of the acts young children create include knife throwing (with imaginary knives), magic disappearing acts, and trick cycling.

At this point, you may wish to demonstrate some simple techniques the students might use, such as working in slow motion, or incorporating a mirror exercise into their act. These early activities are designed to build the children's belief in the drama, to allow them to share their knowledge of circuses with you and the rest of the class, and to give them a sense of ownership of the dramatic context — this is *their* circus community.

For older students (Grade 5 or higher) who may be too self-conscious to undertake these activities, change the key question and the focus of the drama by choosing a viewpoint and context that will engage their interest, enable them to identify with a problem at a feeling level, and challenge their thinking. Ensure that the viewpoint and context you select is not personally threatening to them. For example, older students would probably feel comfortable taking on the roles of a film crew making a documentary about circus life.

After seeking agreement from your students to investigate the ethics surrounding the use of animals in circuses, take the role of the person who commissioned the film. You could say to the class, in role as film-makers, "Good morning, ladies and gentlemen, I am pleased that we have been able to recruit such a talented group of film-makers to undertake this project. To fill you in on some of the details of the documentary you will be making, I would like to spend a little time discussing the project. Please feel free to ask questions and make suggestions, as your ideas are critical to the success of the film."

Stop the drama and allow some time to permit the students to choose and develop their roles as film-makers before proceeding to discuss the content of the film they will make. Planning the drama in this way will permit the class to explore some of the viewpoints and contexts listed above. For example, the film might include shots of the entertainers and trainers rehearsing for the season or neighborhood residents complaining to city council. Exploring different perspectives will require students to take on a variety of roles and to undertake research about circuses. Concurrently, their concentration is focused on the making of the film *about* circuses. This distancing encourages them to reflect on ways in which they can depict circus life with sincerity and honesty.

ACTIVITIES FOR BUILDING BELIEF AND COMMITMENT

Following are some of the activities you can use to build belief in the drama, create a sense of the circus community, and develop some background knowledge about circuses. Further activities may be developed from the viewpoints and contexts listed above.

- Brainstorming different circus acts and listing them.
- Planning the circus on a large sheet of paper.

- Making publicity posters for the circus.
- Students in pairs planning and performing their circus acts, such as miming a high wire act.
- Presenting still images of visitors at opening day at the circus.
- Interviewing different circus members about roles and responsibilities.

At this point in their lives, young students, such as those in Grade 3, have experienced only the pleasures and excitement of the circus. For them to experience a different aspect of circus life as a performer, the teacher could select the viewpoint and context "Entertainers/trainees . . . new arrivals at the circus meet with older members who are faced with lay-offs. Who will have to go?" After the students have shown their acts to each other, the teacher, in role as representative of the owner of the circus, informs them, "Although we are all impressed by the high quality acts that you have prepared for this season, the circus is suddenly faced with great financial difficulties and we cannot afford to keep all of you. Only a few acts will be retained. Today we will have to decide who to keep and who will have to go."

By taking a second-in-command or go-between role, the teacher does not have all the answers to the students' questions, nor is the teacher in a position to make a final decision. Therefore, the teacher can ask the students to suggest how this problem may be resolved so that s/he may take their recommendations to the imaginary owner. This fuses the drama with the tensions of challenge of the unknown and of an obstacle to be overcome. Do not be in a hurry to accept an easy way out, and be prepared to change the attitude of 'the owner'. For example, the owner could become increasingly impatient about the failure to reach a satisfactory decision and deliver an ultimatum through you as his or her representative. The final decision of who will go and who will stay might be influenced by another problem worth exploring in role, such as animal rights activists who protest the presence of performing animals in the circus.

For older students (Grade 5 or higher) who are in role as filmmakers, the drama can be deepened by having them examine the plight of a circus troupe who must defend or justify the continuing use of performing animals. This raises many questions, including, "What will happen to the animals and their

35

trainers?", "Are some animals, such as horses and dogs, suited for circus life?", "Does the use of any animal in circuses dishonor the animal kingdom?"

Planning a role drama for a mining community

TOPIC

A mining community.

SEGMENT THE TOPIC AND IDENTIFY THE LEARNING AREAS

- "Gold fever". How the news of gold discoveries affected people living in far off places. The sort of people that were drawn to the minefields.
- Society in a mining town. How it functioned and how it was held together.
- "Striking it rich." How the sudden discovery of gold altered miners' lives.
- Transportation and communication during a gold rush. How the news was spread, and how aspiring miners reached the minefields.
- The 'boom and bust' mentality. Were the residents of a mining town concerned about building a permanent community?

SELECT THE LEARNING AREA AND FORMULATE A KEY QUESTION

What drew people together and what divided them in their search for gold?

LIST POSSIBLE VIEWPOINTS AND DEFINE CONTEXTS

VIEWPOINTS	POSSIBLE CONTEXTS
Miners	• Examining the contents of the trunks that they brought with them, and showing the various objects to a fellow miner.
	• In years ahead, reflecting on the same articles.
	• Itemizing and listing equipment.

	• Buying supplies at the only store in town, where the prices rise daily.
	• Staking out a claim from a map.
	• Reminiscing about the old days to visitors to the mining ghost town.
Native peoples	• Discovering the loss of traditional hunting grounds.
	• Applying for jobs in the town. Reflecting on what the land was like before the white man arrived.
Government officials/ surveyors/architects	• Planning the townsite.
Government and town officials	• Drawing up rules and regulations for the administration of the townsite.
	• Deciding what form of government is needed for the community.
	• Settling a claim dispute between two miners.
Storekeepers	• Deciding how to stock their stores and what the margin of profit should be.
	• Dealing with overdue debts incurred by miners down on their luck.

Further viewpoints and contexts should be explored to emphasize the contribution of women and visible minorities to the building of the community. To help students shed traditional stereotypical viewpoints, encourage them to assume any role in the drama, regardless of gender, race, or religion. Thus, in this drama, all students could play the roles of the miners' wives, recollecting their feelings when they heard that their husbands had decided to leave for the gold fields. When exploring the perspective of the miners, girls will have the opportunity of taking male roles.

CHOOSE A CONTEXT FOR THE DRAMA AND ROLES FOR YOURSELF
AND STUDENTS

In this drama, the key question, "What drew people together, and what divided them in their search for gold?", might best be answered by planning activities which give students background knowledge about mining communities in the nineteenth century. The viewpoint of "surveyors/government officials/architects" within the context of planning the townsite will require students to have expertise and knowledge about mining towns. This part of the drama can be initiated by finding out from the students what they think they need to know to create a mining town and to draw a plan of it. After the students have done some preliminary research, the teacher can take on the role of 'one seeking information' (in this case as a government representative seeking advice) so that the students are the surveyors and architects who plan the town. To introduce the tension of competition into the drama, divide the class into groups to submit plans for tender. This would be followed by presentations with the use of charts and other drawings. The viewpoint and context would change while each group makes a presentation, placing the remainder of the class in role as government officials and prospective townspeople who are gathered to decide which plan they prefer. Planners are not able to vote for their own plans, and features of several plans may be incorporated in the final plan.

ACTIVITIES FOR BUILDING BELIEF AND COMMITMENT

- In role as surveyors, the students design and map a townsite close to the claims. They submit their plans to government officials, miners, and other townspeople for approval.
- The students, in role as miners and other townspeople, meet with elected town officials to discuss developing laws and regulations to control crime. Should a jail be built? Who should decide how punishment should be administered?
- The owner of the general store is losing money because the miners are experiencing hard times. Students, in role as shareholders in the store, are asked to find a solution.
- There have been a number of attempted robberies at the bank, which has large gold deposits. The students are called in as security experts to upgrade the bank's security system.
- Three people in the town have died from a mysterious disease. The teacher, in role as doctor, is not sure if the sickness is contagious and appeals to the students, in role as townspeople, for help.

- A man is caught cheating in a card game. Later he is discovered murdered. The students, as outside investigators, are called in to reconstruct and solve the crime.
- A TV documentary team wants to film life in a nineteenth-century mining community. Some of the descendants of the original miners help to reconstruct a visual image of what life was like in early days.

Planning a role drama on the effects of a nuclear disaster

TOPIC

An underground community attempts to survive the aftermath of a nuclear disaster.

SEGMENT THE TOPIC AND IDENTIFY THE LEARNING AREAS

- Assessing the damage — the physical and psychological effects of the disaster on the survivors.
- Assuming leadership and taking responsibility — how the new society will be organized and structured and who will make the decisions.
- Retraining the survivors — the education of the people, what skills they will need in the future and what they should remember of the past.
- Living conditions in the underground community — availability of food and water, caring for the sick, combating unknown diseases.

SELECT THE LEARNING AREA AND FORMULATE A KEY QUESTION

How would the survivors find the strength to go on living after a global nuclear explosion, if they were forced to live together underground?

LIST THE POSSIBLE VIEWPOINTS AND DEFINE CONTEXTS

VIEWPOINTS   POSSIBLE CONTEXTS

Survivors   • Planning whether or not to send out an expedition in search of other survivors.

	• Telling stories about the 'old life' and planning for the future.
	• At a group meeting deciding how to organize their society.
Survivors with their families before the disaster	• Planning a Thanksgiving Day reunion, which is scheduled to happen the day after the nuclear explosion.
Child survivors	• In the future, planning a school play about the lives of their grandparents.
Descendants of survivors	• Taking a guided tour of the underground shelter where their ancestors lived.
Future world leaders	• At a summit meeting deciding whether nuclear research should be resumed in the light of increasing world need for energy.
Historians	• Fourth-generation historians (after the nuclear explosion) are commissioned by the authorities to write a slanted perspective extolling life in the underground shelters.
Film crew	• Deciding on key incidents to include in the script for a major film entitled *The Rebirth of Mankind*.

CHOOSE A CONTEXT FOR THE DRAMA AND ROLES FOR YOURSELF
AND STUDENTS

Older students will already have some knowledge and understanding about contemporary problems. In this drama, the teacher may wish to discuss ways in which a global nuclear disaster could occur, mindful of the fact that this might be an environmental accident and not an act of war.

After brainstorming different possibilities, divide the students into groups of five or six to create a tableau showing what happened minutes after the explosion.

Use of the tableau in this way reveals the students' present understandings of the effects of nuclear explosions and is a powerful mode of learning for other members of the class. While the teacher and the rest of the class study each tableau, the teacher can ask the observing students to give a title to the picture, say aloud the thoughts of various characters in the tableau, and describe what they think was happening before the explosion. Students will want to say what is happening in each tableau, but don't be in a hurry to conduct a guessing game. The entire group of tableaux will collectively create a composite image of what occurred after the explosion and will provide the class with a vivid and absorbing start to their drama.

The various tableaux also provide a wealth of opportunities for further exploration. For example, the teacher could ask students to choose the tableau that makes them wonder the most about surviving a nuclear disaster. The class can then create a drama about one group of people whose lives are totally altered by the explosion. On the other hand, all the tableaux could be displayed in a museum of the future, commemorating this global disaster. In role as historians of the future, the students could attempt to reconstruct the events that led to the explosion. Always the objective in this kind of drama is to encourage students to explore and depict the forces that influence events rather than merely to show the events themselves.

The following section describes a number of activities which may help plan a drama on this topic. Although less use has been made of teacher in role in this drama, the teacher still has an important part to play in helping the students to structure their work to deepen their understanding of the key question and its resulting issues. Even though the teacher may not be in role, the questions should be as penetrating and reflective as if s/he were actually taking part.

ACTIVITIES FOR BUILDING BELIEF AND COMMITMENT

- Survivors create tableaux of what they were doing when the explosion occurred. The teacher asks the survivors to step out of their tableaux to tell what is happening.
- Students trace the past life of one of the survivors depicted in the tableaux: class constructs snapshots of this survivor's life.
- After the initial shock of the explosion, survivors gather to draw up plans for survival and for organizing their society.
- After the underground community is organized, a few go above ground. Interviews by reporters of what they found. Their feelings about the changes.

- Survivors keep a day-to-day written record of their life underground.
- Each survivor talks to a friend about one article s/he has saved that has special significance to him/her.
- One 'cell' of survivors with a secret cache of food is visited by a survivor (teacher in role) from a 'cell' with little or no food. Should they trust this person?

Conclusion

A common thread of building a community has run through these various plans for role drama. Drama is a collective learning experience in which individuals are given the opportunity to make individual choices, test their ideas, and take risks in what Dorothy Heathcote (1984) calls a "no penalty area."

The more regularly you use drama in the classroom, the more comfortable you and your students will feel working in role. We recommend, therefore, that you use some of the activities described here in daily 10- to 15-minute sessions for younger students (Grades 3 and 4), and 30-minute sessions or longer for older students (Grades 5 to 9). Older students will need more time to discuss and reflect on their work. As you become more confident working in role, you will probably want to extend the time of your sessions.

Selected references

Byron, Ken. "Indians and Pioneers." In 2D Drama Teaching Resource Pack No. 1, *2D Journal*, Leicester, England, 1985.

Cazden, Courtnay. *Classroom Discourse*. Cambridge: Cambridge University Press, 1988.

Heathcote, Dorothy. "Material for Significance." In *Dorothy Heathcote: Collected Writings on Education and Drama*, edited by Liz Johnson and Cecily O'Neill. London: Hutchinson, 1984.

Morgan, Norah, and Juliana Saxton. *Teaching Drama: A Mind of Many Wonders*. London: Hutchinson, 1987.

Neelands, Jonothan. *Structuring Drama Work*. New York: Cambridge University Press, 1990.

3

··············

Creating your own story

Chapters 3, 4, and 5 contain detailed descriptions of role dramas that have actually occurred in classrooms and which may provide a guide for teachers in their own planning. *These are not lesson plans but descriptions of actual lessons.* Teachers, therefore, should use them as a guide, adapting the steps in any way necessary.

To assist teachers in their planning, an outline of each set of lessons is provided at the beginning of each chapter.

This chapter describes a role drama that springs from a story created by Patrick Verriour. "The Fierce Dragon," based on the traditional idea of a village that is threatened by a dragon, demonstrates how you can create your own stories as a stimulus for role drama. Teachers often feel that they have to search out a perfect story, when, if they keep in mind that the best stories for drama have an interesting issue and a group of people to grapple with that issue, they can readily create their own.

Time frame and grade level

This role drama was carried out in four sessions over a seven-hour period. The first two sessions were ninety minutes each, and the last two were two hours long.

Remember that you can break the sessions into smaller units. It is simply a matter of finding the right time to stop. Conversely, if the interest is high, you can make your sessions longer.

The description that follows is of a Grade 4 class at work.

However, the drama may be done similarly with Grades 5, 6 and 7, and, with some modification, could be adapted for primary grades as well.

Teaching strategies

The following outline shows the teacher's planning for this role drama:

SESSION ONE

> Discussing in large group
> Telling the story
> Questioning
> Discussing
> Writing

SESSION TWO

> Discussing
> Teacher and students in role as villagers
> Guided imagery
> Storytelling in pairs
> Tableaux

SESSION THREE

> Choosing a name for the village
> Teacher in role as a reporter
> Discussing out of role
> Discussing in small groups
> Reporting to large group
> Writing the message

SESSION FOUR

> Discussing in small groups
> Creating tableaux
> Reading the tableaux
> Writing stories
> Reading stories and discussing them

Session one

To start the drama, the teacher talks to the class about fear, then asks them to form into small groups of three or four to discuss the following:

• What kinds of things are people afraid of?
• What do people do when they are afraid?

Each group is asked to choose one person to report to the class after the discussion. In answer to the first question, the students make a number of suggestions that include things that are physically threatening as well as those that are imaginary. The class feels that most people run away or try to hide from things that scare them.

Note: This is what this class offered when faced with this question. It is not "the right answer" that a teacher should lead the class to. The questions are part of the teacher's planning. The answers will vary, depending on the group's thinking.

TELLING THE STORY

The Fierce Dragon

Once upon a time a terrible and frightening dragon descended on a peaceful country where the people had never seen a dragon before. He had clearly come to stay, for he dug himself a deep cave in the mountain nearby and set up house. Breathing fire, he roared out to the people of the country to listen to him.

"All you people, mark my words and mark them well. Now that I have come to live with you, I will need food. I shall expect you to pay me a tribute of cows, lambs, and pigs. If you obey me, you will live, but if anyone fails to pay me, I shall eat that person."

The people were very frightened and soon began giving the dragon all the animals that he could eat. This went on for quite a long time until there were no animals left to bring to the dragon. The once peaceful and prosperous country lay in ruins. The people were now very poor. They had nothing for themselves, let alone the dragon. But he didn't go away. Instead he started flying around, swooping down on people, carrying them away to his cave in his enormous claws. There he devoured them. The

45

poor villagers were very frightened. They were desperate to find a way of getting rid of the dragon.

QUESTIONING

The teacher stops at this point in the story to tell the class that the first part of the drama will be taking place in the village. Questions are asked to build up a group picture of the village.

Comment: As so little of the story has actually been told, the students are encouraged to think inferentially. In addition, the students are required to listen carefully to one another, to make compromises, and to reach agreement about the sort of village they will create.

DISCUSSING

The students decide that the drama will be about a village set four hundred years ago. Most of the villagers are farmers, although there are some skilled tradespeople. Because the dragon has been demanding a regular tribute, the village is poor and its citizens are scared and confused. Through the discussion, the class develops a collective image of a small village with simple houses. The students have some problems conceptualizing a village of four centuries ago, so one child suggests that it could be like a Haida village which they have been studying in social studies. The other children agree with this suggestion.

Again, this is what this group of young people offered. The teacher is not looking for any particular type of village, but is willing to accept and work with what the young people offer.

WRITING

The lesson concludes with the children writing a short description of the village and its inhabitants.

Session two
DISCUSSING

To assess the understanding and the commitment of the students, the teacher talks about the issues and events of the last session, asking, "What do you remember about our village? How are the villagers feeling about the presence of the dragon?" The group discusses these questions.

Comment: Even though it has been a week since the last session, the students still have a clear picture of the village and the feelings of the villagers. This is not unusual. Students regularly remember and fall into role in each of the five weekly sessions. Were they to forget what they had been doing, it would be a sure sign that they had lost interest. In that case, the teacher should stop the drama and go on to something new.

TEACHER AND STUDENTS IN ROLE AS VILLAGERS

The students are asked to sit in a circle. The teacher says, "Imagine that we are those villagers, sitting together in the village square. They are meeting to talk about the dragon and the way it has changed their lives. I think it would be a good idea for each villager to begin with the words, 'Since the dragon came to our village. . . .' I'll begin, and we can go around the circle so that each villager can have a say about how the dragon has changed his or her life."

The teacher then says, "Since the dragon came to this village, I'm afraid to leave my house. I can't get any chores done, and the farm is a mess."

Comment: Teacher modeling is very important. First, it reinforces the language pattern that the teacher is asking for. It also shows that the teacher is willing to make a serious commitment to a role along with the students. If the teacher tackles this task with commitment, the children will follow suit.

Among the students' contributions in role are:

- The animals won't eat or leave the barns. They are getting sick and might die.
- The chickens won't lay eggs anymore and the cows won't give any milk.
- My children are afraid to go to school.
- My husband won't leave the house.
- I'm afraid all the time. My children hide under the bed. They won't come out.

When all the children have spoken, the teacher says, "The dragon has ruined this town. The only happy times I have now are when I can remember how life used to be here before this dragon came. Do you remember how good things were before?" Several children nod agreement.

GUIDED IMAGERY

The teacher asks the students to close their eyes and remember what life was like before the dragon came. "Take yourself back to a time before the dragon came to this village. Focus in on a specific time that you can remember. It may have been a special occasion or a very ordinary day. Remember what kind of day or night it was. Was it a warm sunny time or a crisp autumn time, or perhaps it was winter or spring. Fix the day and the time in your mind. Look around. Who is there with you? Where are you? Are you in your home, out in the garden, working on the farm, or in the village? Think of the place and who is there with you. Of course, you could be alone too. What are you doing? If there are other people there, what are they doing? See yourself and what is happening."

The teacher waits for a while and then asks the children to open their eyes.

STORYTELLING IN PAIRS

The teacher asks the students to work in pairs and exchange the stories that they have just imagined. While the students do this, the teacher circulates, listening to the stories and asking questions to deepen the children's thinking.

TABLEAUX

The children are asked to work in groups to create a tableau that shows what life was like before the dragon came. The children set to work and produce tableaux which show families having picnics together in the fields, harvesting crops, gossiping together in the market square, making bread, and milking cows.

All the tableaux are shown at once. The teacher then asks each group to freeze in its tableau as the class 'reads' them.

Comment: Guided imagery, talking, and then making tableaux which are discussed are valuable prewriting activities. If the teacher wishes, this could be a good time for the children to write stories of what the village was like before the dragon came. These could be collated into a published book which could be part of the history of this village.

Session three
CHOOSING A NAME FOR THE VILLAGE

At the start of this activity, the teacher asks the class, "What shall we call this village that we have created?" After some discussion, a student suggests Willowbrook. The class unanimously accepts this name.

TEACHER IN ROLE AS REPORTER

The teacher talks briefly about the first session and how it was concerned with life before the dragon came. She then tells the group that they are to imagine that they are now at the time when the dragon has taken much of their food. The villagers are now poor and frightened. The dragon is terrorizing everybody. The teacher tells them that a reporter has come to Willowbrook to interview the villagers about the fearful dragon. The teacher, in role as reporter, approaches one of the students.

Reporter: How long have you lived in Willowbrook?
Villager: All my life.
Reporter: Is it true that there is a dragon that is actually eating people around here?
Villager: Yes.
Reporter: I find that difficult to believe. Could you tell me about that?

The villagers begin to tell their stories about the dragon. One woman says that her six children have all been killed by the dragon. The reporter needs a lot of convincing to believe in this dragon but is finally convinced by the earnestness of the villagers.

Comment: Because the teacher, in role as reporter, is skeptical, the children, in role as villagers, have to work very hard, describing the events that have taken place in their village.

49

They employ the language of argument and description to convince this skeptic. Because so much time has been spent in building-belief activities, the group's belief in their village is strong and their arguments persuasive. The reporter is impressed.

The reporter asks for eyewitness accounts of the dragon. The villagers are asked to give a detailed description of the dragon. One suggests that the dragon is black and green with a long scaly tail. The other villagers add to this: smoke-filled nostrils, fire-red eyes, sharp teeth and claws. The reporter takes notes on all this, then asks, "What are you going to do about the dragon?"

The children are surprised by this. They were enthusiastically describing the dragon and were enjoying this. No one speaks. The teacher, in role as reporter, says, "Well? Surely you aren't going to just sit around and do nothing until you starve to death or are eaten by this monster, are you? You have to do something."

Silence. Finally, one boy says, "What can we do?"

The teacher, in role as reporter, replies, "I don't know, but then I don't live here. It really isn't my problem. But if I did live here, I'm sure I'd think of something."

One student says, "But he's stronger than we are."

Another adds, "He's got sharp claws."

The teacher, in role as reporter, shrugs.

Comment: The teacher, in role as reporter, doesn't give an opinion when asked, "What can we do?" She gives the problem back to the children to solve, making sure they grapple with this and thus are the ones doing the thinking and learning.

DISCUSSING OUT OF ROLE

The class seems to be at a loss. The teacher says, "Well now, I guess that reporter is quite right. Something should be done, but what? It's a difficult situation, isn't it? The villagers were quite right. He is stronger and he does have sharp claws. Perhaps we should work in small groups of four. In your groups, see if you can come up with some possible solutions to this dilemma. Make someone the reporter in your group. He or she can bring your ideas back to the class later. Okay?"

Comment: Here the teacher chooses to have the class discuss

this out of role. She acknowledges that it is a difficult problem. She could have kept the students in role, but when students are at a real loss, it is sometimes better to take them out of role, acknowledge how difficult the problem is, discuss it, and then go back into role.

DISCUSSING IN SMALL GROUPS

The children break into groups and begin discussing what to do. The teacher circulates, asking questions where necessary. The questions centre around opening up the implications of their suggestions. For example, when one group suggests moving out of the area, the teacher asks, "Where will we go and how will we get away? We'll be prime targets leaving, won't we?" Someone suggests digging a tunnel to escape through. The teacher says, "Yes, that could work, although it would be very laborious. I wonder how long it would take? And where will we end up?"

Comment: Although the groups are out of role, most of the students speak as if they are still in role. This shows that they are very much operating in "now time." They have developed a belief in and a commitment to these villagers and their problems.

REPORTING TO LARGE GROUP

The large group reconvenes and suggestions for dealing with the dragon are presented. Among these are:

- Get the army to attack him.
- Leave the town secretly in the middle of the night or dig a tunnel to leave by.
- Send out a message to see if there are any dragon slayers who could come and kill the dragon.
- Meet with the dragon to try and reason with him.
- Put poison in the animals that he is eating.
- Do some research on how to get rid of dragons.

After a spirited discussion, the group finally decides to send out a message to a dragon slayer.

WRITING THE MESSAGE

The group decides to write letters to the mayors of neighboring towns, asking them if they know of any dragon slayer who could get rid of their dragon. As a group, they discuss what kind of information is necessary to go into the letter. They then write the letters.

Session four
DISCUSSING IN SMALL GROUP

The teacher asks the students to work in small groups to discuss what happens next and to suggest how the drama could conclude. The students in each group share their ideas with each other. Most groups agree that the dragon slayer comes and quickly dispatches the dragon.

The teacher asks: "How does it happen?" The group offers suggestions.

CREATING TABLEAUX

The teacher suggests that the class work in groups of five to create the story of how the dragon slayer rids the town of the dragon. The groups are to decide on the story first and then plan a series of six tableaux to tell the story. The tableaux will be prepared, the story told, then presented to the class in a series. The class will close their eyes, the group will form its first tableau, and then the teacher will tell the class to reopen their eyes. When the teacher tells the class to close their eyes again, the group will have five seconds to form the next tableau. Then the class will reopen their eyes, and so on until all the tableaux from each group are presented.

Comment: This exercise is very effective. It is important that the students keep their eyes closed between each tableau or else the effect is spoiled.

The students work on their stories and their tableaux. The teacher circulates to make sure that there are no difficulties.

READING THE TABLEAUX

The class is given about twenty minutes to complete this task.

Then the first group presents its story in stills. The audience 'reads' the stills and discusses each one. Questions are asked if there are any stills that are unclear.

The group described on these pages has no difficulty in showing their stories. The tableaux are 'readable' and different. The stories range from the predictable (the dragon slayer attacks and after a series of horrible struggles manages to triumph over the dragon, killing it) to the unusual. At the end of each group's work, there is discussion of what the audience 'read.'

One group presents an unusual series, using most of its members to be the dragon. The smallest member of the group is chosen to be the dragon slayer. In the first still he peeps from behind a rock, while the dragon sleeps. In the second still he stands before the dragon which is now awake and surprised. The young dragon slayer looks tough and brave. In the third, the dragon and the slayer appear to be talking earnestly. The dragon looks a little suspicious; the slayer looks confident. The fourth still reveals the dragon looking sheepish and the slayer obviously lecturing him. By the fifth, the dragon is in tears, lying helplessly on the ground, while the slayer continues to lecture. The sixth still shows the dragon with his back to the slayer, obviously leaving, looking most dejected, while the slayer waves a triumphant goodbye!

At the end of this series of stills, the teacher says, "Well, it seems that that dragon slayer was somehow able to shame the dragon into leaving. I wonder what he said to the dragon that was so effective?"

The students are bubbling with ideas as to what he could have said. The group who created this series is dying to tell the real story, but the teacher says that for now it is better not to know, but rather to wonder.

WRITING STORIES

After all the stills have been seen, the teacher says, "I wonder how those villagers put their lives back together after the dragon was actually gone? In many ways it would be like putting your life together after a war, a flood, an earthquake, or some major disaster. I suppose it takes a long time to really recover.

Let us suppose that a week has passed since the dragon was

disposed of. It doesn't really matter which of the stories we have seen was true. You can pick one of them or combine some if you like, or make up a new story. Sit down in your house, safe now from the terrors of the dragon, and write a letter to someone very close to you who doesn't live in your village, telling that person about what has happened and how the dragon was disposed of." The children write.

READING THE STORIES AND DISCUSSING THEM

When the stories are finished, they are circulated and discussed in small groups. A book is made of the stories for the class library.

Selected references

Lattimore, Deborah. *The Dragon's Robe*. New York: Harper and Row, 1991.

Wallace, Ian. *Chin Chiang and the Dragon's Dance*. Vancouver: Douglas & McIntyre, 1984.

4
....

Folktale source — "Rumplestiltskin"

In this chapter, another role drama is described in detail. Although based on the folktale "Rumplestiltskin," the story was changed to allow for a group entry. The dilemma of the story remains the same, but by inventing a role for the Advisors, the teacher is able to provide parts for all students in the class, allowing everyone to enter into the story and grapple with the Queen's problem.

Time frame and grade level

The drama described in this chapter was done in five sessions of approximately one and a half hours each. However, the time frame is flexible. Sometimes a drama can be carried on for 20 hours or more if the interest is high and new learning areas occur. Also, this drama can be done in one session of one and a half hours.

This description is of a Grade 6 class at work. It is not intended to be a lesson plan, but is an actual description of what occurred in classrooms. The same drama can be done with any level of students. The same language and the same approach can be used no matter what grade you are working with. In the primary grades, the idea of jumping into and out of role is not foreign at all, for small children naturally play that way. With older students, a more academic approach can be taken. Before the storytelling, talk about folktales, discussing the fact that many of the same tales appear in a variety of cultures, and discuss the universal issues they contain. With older students, you may wish to spend more time researching and discussing the implications of events. However, the basic structure is the same.

Teaching strategies

The following outline shows the teacher's planning for this role drama:

SESSION ONE

Telling the story
Posing a question to wonder about
Explaining working in role and seeking agreement
Students think while teacher questions
Pair interviewing
Reporting back
Pair interviewing
Teacher in role, questioning
Still image, demonstrated by teacher and 'read' by students
Students create a still image, 'read' by teacher

SESSION TWO

Imaging the room
Drawing the room and writing a description

SESSION THREE

Setting up the room physically
Finding a way of sitting and standing
Still image while teacher narrates
Speaking thoughts out loud
Meeting of the Queen and her Advisors
The script
Planning
Writing in role as Advisors
Classifying the written responses
Reflecting on the drama

Session one

TELLING THE STORY

The Story of Jack Simpson

Once there was a Miller and his beautiful daughter. They lived in a small cottage at the edge of a leafy, green forest. They were not rich. They didn't have many material possessions. But they lived simple lives and were fairly happy.

One day when the Miller was at work, he happened to glance out of his window and to his amazement he saw the King's hunting party with the King himself, riding toward his cottage! They were a magnificent sight. If you can imagine, there were thirty of the King's best huntsmen riding on the best horses that the Royal stables had to offer. The horses' coats gleamed in the sunlight. They had been brushed until they shone! Each horse had its own saddle cloth that had been embroidered in gold and silver with the King's very own monogram. The saddles were made of the finest leather and they too had been polished until they shone. Each huntsman was wearing long boots, made of the softest leather, which came up to his knees, and each wore breeches made of the softest velvet. Matching their breeches were coats also made of soft velvet and these were either green like the forest itself, or royal red, the King's favorite color. On their heads they wore soft hats and from each dangled a plume. The Miller gasped in astonishment, so impressive a sight were they. He was even more amazed when he saw them stop outside his humble cottage and the King himself dismounted and knocked on his door!

The Miller ran to open it and the King walked right into his tiny kitchen and sat down. "My good man," the King began, "my horses need water. We have come a long way and they are thirsty. Could you attend to them please?" Of course the Miller did as he was asked and ran around trying to make himself useful. While the King was there, he couldn't help but notice the Miller's beautiful daughter.

The Miller was very nervous having the King in his cottage, and in his nervousness he did something very stupid. He told the King a lie. And it was this. He told the King that his daughter was not only beautiful but clever as well. In fact, he told him, she was so clever that she could take ordinary old bits of straw and spin them on a spinning wheel until they changed into gold.

Of course the King was very interested in this, and he told the Miller to come to his Palace the next morning, and to bring his daughter.

The next morning when they arrived, the King requested that they stay with him for a few days and he took the Miller's daughter by the hand and led her down the stone corridor of the Palace and up three stone stairs until they came to a room. He pushed open the door and she saw that in the room there were only two things, a spinning wheel and a pile of old straw.

"Miller's daughter," the King said, "take this straw and spin it into gold for me by tomorrow and if you don't, then tomorrow you will die." Then he left.

The young woman was distraught. How could she do what he asked? She didn't have the faintest idea how. She was so upset that she began to cry. Suddenly the door opened, and a young man appeared in the room.

"Who are you?" she asked.

'My name is Jack Simpson," the young man replied. "Can I be of help?"

"Be of help?" replied the distraught young woman. "Yes, if you know how to spin straw into gold you can help, but nobody can do that." And she began to weep again.

"I can," replied Jack cheerfully, "and I'll do it for you if you give me that necklace you're wearing."

"Of course," she replied as she handed Jack the necklace.

Whirr whirr whirr whirr . . . one bobbin full of gold. Whirr, whirr, whirr . . . two bobbins full of gold. And in the morning there were 68 bobbins full of gold gleaming in the sun as Jack took his leave. The King came down. Now he was a very avaricious type and when he saw these bobbins full of gold his greedy eyes lit up with glee and he was very pleased.

He took the young woman by the hand, led her along the stone corridor of the Palace and up another two stone steps to a room like the other. Inside, there was just a big heap of straw and another spinning wheel.

"Take all this straw and spin it into gold or tomorrow you will die!" he ordered. Then he went away. The young woman was now more distressed than ever. She didn't know what to do. She didn't know where Jack Simpson was and she had no idea whether he would come again. Finally she became so distraught that she began to weep. While she was crying, the door opened and Jack Simpson entered.

"Oh, Mr. Simpson, I am so glad that you have come. Could you take all this straw and spin it into gold for me again, please?"

"Certainly, but if I do, would you give me that ring you're wearing?"

"Gladly," answered the Miller's daughter, and she gave Jack her ring as he sat down at the spinning wheel. Whirr, whirr, whirr, whirr . . . one bobbin full of gold! Well, you know the rest. In the morning when Jack left there were 79 bobbins full of gold gleaming in the sunshine.

The avaricious king arrived and his avaricious eyes lit up with glee. He was very pleased. He took the young woman by the hand and took her to yet another room in the Palace where there were just two things. You guessed it! Just one spinning wheel and an even bigger pile of straw than before.

The King spoke. "Miller's daughter, may I call you Sasha (for that was her name)? I am very impressed by you. You are very beautiful and very clever and I've grown fond of you. Tomorrow after you have turned this straw into gold I will marry you and make you my Queen. We will rule over this kingdom together and you will have anything your heart desires — brocade and silk dresses, servants to wait on you, jewels, French champagne on special occasions, carriages, pearls, diamonds! But of course, if you fail to spin this straw into gold, then tomorrow you will die." And he went away.

Poor Sasha, she was very distraught but hoped that Jack would come and rescue her. So she waited, and the clock ticked on and ten o'clock came but no Jack, and eleven o'clock came and went. By midnight she was very distressed and began crying again when suddenly, about one-thirty, the door opened and there stood Jack Simpson. Sasha was overjoyed to see him.

"Thank heavens you have come, Mr. Simpson. Please, begin spinning. There isn't much time!"

59

"Certainly. What will you give this time?"

Sasha stopped and was very still. Alas, she had nothing to give him. She was a poor person with very few material possessions.

"Oh," she cried, "I have nothing. I gave you the ring my mother gave me and the necklace my grandmother left me. Alas, I have nothing left. And she began to weep, more copiously than before.

Jack spoke. "If I spin this straw then you will become Queen, isn't that right? And then you could give me anything I wanted."

"Of course. Why didn't I think of that? Yes. Help me now and then I can give you anything you want when I am Queen, anything."

"Good. I will do this for you if you will promise me that when you become Queen and have your first child, you will give the child to me. Is it agreed?"

"Of course!" agreed the young woman. "Whatever you want. Only please begin!"

You see, she didn't know what she was saying. She didn't even know whether she would have a child. She agreed without thinking. Jack sat down at the spinning wheel. Whirr, whirr, whirr, whirr . . . one bobbin full of gold. He kept spinning through the night and before he left in the morning, there were 122 bobbins full of gold!

The avaricious King arrived and was very pleased. And he kept his promise. He married Sasha and she became Queen. Even though he was avaricious, he had some good points and they actually had quite a good marriage. About a year after the wedding, Queen Sasha gave birth to a baby girl. She was christened Princess Patricia and the whole kingdom rejoiced. The young Queen had forgotten all about Jack Simpson and her promise. She was very happy and enjoyed being a mother. One day, when the baby was about a year old, she was playing with her in the nursery when suddenly the door opened and in walked Jack Simpson. He said, "Your Majesty, I've come for the baby."

The Queen didn't know what to say. Finally she managed, "What do you mean, you've come for the baby?"

"Remember, Your Majesty, that I did a very great favor for you and in return you promised me your first child. Here I am. I've come for it."

The Queen was very upset. She remembered that she had promised, but she didn't want to keep her promise.

"Could you just let me have the baby for another three days?" she asked. "It is so hard to say goodbye. I need time."

"Certainly," said Jack. "I am a reasonable man. I'll return in three days." And he left.

The young Queen was more distraught than she had ever been. What could she do? She didn't want to give Jack her baby, but she had promised him, that was true. The King was away on a hunting trip and she had no one to turn to. She walked up and down in her chambers half the night, weeping and worrying. And then, about three o'clock in the morning when she was quite exhausted, she suddenly remembered. Now that she was Queen, she didn't have to solve problems on her own. She had in the Palace a group of Royal Advisors. It was their job to advise her on any matter which caused her difficulty. And they were clever people, who had all been to university! They knew lots of things. All she had to do was tell them what the problem was, and they would tell her what to do. She would call a meeting in the morning. This made her feel much better and she promptly fell asleep.

POSING A QUESTION TO WONDER ABOUT

Teacher: "I wonder what they told her to do. Would you like to find out?"

Comment: I have told this story to over 6,000 people, ranging in age from six to sixty. I have *never* had a group that was indifferent to the dilemma. The usual response is an enthusiastic "Yes!" because the problem is universally intriguing. The issue of whether this young mother should honor her promise and give away her child interests people of any age. It is a classic dilemma.

EXPLAINING WORKING IN ROLE AND SEEKING AGREEMENT

Teacher: "We can find out by doing something called 'working in role'. Here's how it works. I will agree to take on the role of that Queen and think like her (and that's difficult for me, because I've never been a Queen and I'm not that young anymore), if you will agree to take on the role of those Royal Advisors and think like them. Would you agree to that?"

Comment: The teacher's language is very important here. She is making a *contract* with the young people, asking them to agree to certain terms. She is agreeing to do something if they will agree to something. This is a collaboration, an important aspect of working in role drama.

If the students seem reluctant, the teacher must assure them of help in this difficult task. And it *is* difficult, especially if the children are small. They are going to be required to take on the roles of educated adults and try to think like them.

It is frequently helpful to acknowledge that the task is difficult. The teacher may say something like, "I know this is difficult for you too, because you haven't been adults yet, and you may think it will be hard to think like them. Would you be willing to have a try at it?" If, however, the young people do not show any hesitation in tackling this task, don't talk about difficulty, just plunge in.

STUDENTS THINK / TEACHER QUESTIONS

Teacher: "Well, we need to do a bit of thinking about this first. Now, I don't know if you realize this, but all leaders throughout history have had advisors. These people, men and women, are experts who know a lot about their subjects. They have studied for many years. Most of them have been to university for a long time. So, I am going to ask you to just think alone for a moment. Say to yourself, 'If I am an adult advisor to the Queen, I wonder how old I am. I must be old enough to have finished university and, of course, young enough to still be working'. Pick a specific age. Not *around* 30 or maybe 21, but a *specific* age."

Comment: It is worth while spending some time at this point, as it is important that the students do not treat choosing an age lightly, such as an age of 150 or more. It is also important that they do realize that they are adults so that a very young age is equally not suitable. A sixteen-year-old would not have had the training and the experience necessary for a very important job. The students should be made aware that we are trying to be as much like the real world as possible in this kind of drama. That is why they will like working this way.

I once had a group in which a boy decided he was 80, and the class initially dismissed this as an unsuitable age. They insisted he was too old for the job. They debated it for quite a long time, making the observing teachers very impatient. They couldn't understand why I didn't just stop the students and settle the argument. However, the level of debate was high, and while only two boys were doing most of the talking, the rest of the group were listening with interest. It isn't often that students get the opportunity to hear a quality debate. As well, if you really believe in handing over the power to the students, then you must be prepared to give them the time to work and decide things. This debate finally ended when the boy who was opting to be 80 said, "Look, we're not choosing a baseball team here. We are choosing an age for a thinker! Have you ever heard of Einstein? He was one of the greatest thinkers and he was still thinking okay when he was 80. That's the kind of eighty-year-old I'm gonna be!" No problem. He was 80. The class had heard a quality debate. The boy had settled it with the class instead of the teacher imposing her will, and we'd all been given something to think about.

The teacher continues the questioning that guides the students into imaging their roles: "How long have you been doing this job? How did you get it? What things do you know about? What things did you study at university which equip you for this very important job? Where do you live in the Palace? What is your room like? Who lives there with you? Don't forget that if you are an adult you may be married and have children. If you are over 40, you could be a grandparent. What are the names of the people in your family? What are the ages of the children, if there are any? What is your average day like? What time do you get up? When does the Queen have meetings — every day? once a week? only when there are important problems to be discussed? What kind of food do you eat? What things do you do when you aren't working? What kind of hobbies do you have? Remember the story takes place quite a long time ago, before TV and computers or even electric lights. I wonder how those people entertained themselves."

Comment: Allow time between these questions, so that the young people have a chance to think. This questioning should push them into thinking specifically about themselves as Advisors and the kind of life they would live. Imaging in detail will help build a commitment to the drama and will discourage superficial thinking.

PAIR INTERVIEWING

Teacher: "We'll work in pairs. Could you find someone to work with and sit down when you have. Don't sit down until you have a partner."

Comment: This is an efficient way for the teacher to see who is left over. She can quickly pair up those who are left.

The teacher instructs: "Say to your partner, 'I'll be an A and you be a B.' Hands up, all the As. (Teacher can check quickly that there is just one A in each pair.) Good. Hands up, all the Bs.

As, just for a minute, I want you to forget about being an advisor. You are a reporter. You have been sent to interview a Royal Advisor to the Queen. You must find out everything you can about that person. For example, if I were working with this person here (teacher chooses a student close by) and I were the person interviewing, I would do something like this."

The teacher mimes turning a page in a stenographer's notepad. "Good morning, sir, I believe you work in the Palace as a Royal Advisor. Is that right? How long have you been working there?"

After the teacher has demonstrated with a few questions, she congratulates the student she was working with for being able to think well on his feet, then addresses the whole class again. "Don't forget to find out what your Advisor studied at university and anything else you can find out about the Advisors' lives up there in the Palace."

Students begin their interviewing.

Comment: By demonstrating briefly to the students, the teacher is able to show commitment to the task, demonstrating that it is to be done seriously, as much like a real reporter as possible. While the students are interviewing each other, the teacher circulates, listening to the kinds of questions that are being asked. It is difficult for young people to know what kinds of questions to ask to get the kind of information they need. If a pair is having trouble, the teacher suggests ideas such as, "Have you found out what this Advisor does when he/she isn't working? Ask the person to describe his/her room to you in detail. How is it furnished? Is there a view from the window? Describe the view."

REPORTING BACK

After sufficient time has been allowed for the interviewing, the teacher says, "Could all the interviewers stand please. I am going to ask you to tell us one thing that you learned from your interview. Be selective. I know you learned a lot of things, but just pick the one thing which you think is the most interesting." (The teacher chooses one of the students standing.) "What was the most interesting thing you learned?"

Each student describes one interesting thing. From this information, a collective picture emerges of the Advisors and their lives in the Palace.

PAIR INTERVIEWING

The teacher then asks the Bs to take on the role of reporter and find out everything they can about their partner, the Royal Advisor. As before, the teacher circulates, helping by modeling questions where necessary.

TEACHER IN ROLE, QUESTIONING

After sufficient time has been allowed for the interviewing, the teacher asks the Bs to stand. S/he then goes into role, addressing the first one, "I hear you've been up at the Palace talking to those Royal Advisors. I heard that they aren't a very intelligent lot. Did you get that impression?"

Comment: Going into role like this will surprise the interviewers who will be expecting to be asked to report in the same way that the As were. Answering this type of question presses them to think at a different level, and quickly too. They are being asked to judge the character of the person they have interviewed rather than just reporting what they have heard. *Surprise* is one of the basic elements of drama. It creates interest and tension, which makes things exciting. I have never come across students who could not rise to the demand made by this kind of question, even though they are always surprised.

Students say things like, "Well, I don't know, I thought the Advisor I spoke with was very intelligent." Or, "That's right. He did seem pretty dumb to me."

Comment: The teacher continues this line of questioning, asking questions which demand a creative type of thinking from the student. "I heard that they didn't really work all that hard up there. Was that your impression? Is it true that they get the jobs because they have connections, relatives with power and things? I heard that these Advisors didn't really know much at all. Is it true that they spend most of their time just loafing about? Would you trust the Advisor you spoke with? I mean, did he seem honest to you?"

The following is a transcript from an actual session of "The Story of Jack Simpson," illustrating a typical exchange between teacher and Grade 6 students at this stage of the session.

Teacher (to Student 1): I hear you've just come from interviewing one of those Royal Advisors at the Palace. Is that right?
Student 1: That's right.
T: I heard they were a lazy bunch on the whole. They don't do much. Is that right?
S1: Well, not really, I mean they don't have a lot to do.
T: Just loaf around all day?
S1: Well, they have meetings.
T: Not many though.
S1: Well, when they do have them, they work hard at solving problems.
T: That's not very hard work, though, is it?
S1: It isn't easy.
T: Are you saying they do work hard then? They're conscientious?
S1: Yes, I'd say they do work fairly hard.
T: Conscientious?
S1: Yes.
T: Well, what do you know? That's different from what I've heard.
(To Student 2): Was that your impression, that they were a conscientious lot? I mean, did they seem to be hard workers to you?
S2: Not really. I didn't talk with them all or anything, but the Advisor I spoke with seemed pretty lazy, not conscientious at all.
T: Yes, see? That's what I heard too.
(To Student 3): Was that your impression?
S3: My Advisor works really hard. She has meetings night and day.
T: Really? What about?

S3: Umm, er. . . lot's of problems. (Pause) The Advisors have to solve lots of problems, you know. I think they work hard, or at least the one I spoke to did.

T: Interesting.

(To Student 4): Someone told me that many of them weren't all that trustworthy. What was your impression? Did you find the Advisor you spoke to was a trustworthy type?

S4: I guess so.

T: Well, did you feel you could trust him, for example?

S4: Yeah.

T: How come?

S4: What?

T: Well, what made you feel you could trust him?

S4: I don't know. He seemed honest. I believed what he said. He said that he only met with the Queen once a day, but he did other things as well, study and stuff.

T: Oh.

(To Student 5): What was your experience?

Comment: As can be seen by the above exchange, the students and teacher are in a dialogue which pushes them further in their thinking. As well, the teacher is using a word like 'conscientious' in such a way that the meaning is clear. Student 2 then uses the word in her dialogue with the teacher. Although there is no way of knowing whether this is a new word for the student, experience suggests that students will use words that the teacher has used minutes before, if the word is used in a way which makes its meaning clear. Language is learned in context and the teacher should consciously upgrade the language in the classroom wherever possible.

The teacher is in role with the students during this exchange but has not explained who she is. In fact, the teacher is playing the role of someone who seeks information. She could be a neighbor or a fellow reporter. It is not necessary to explain the role to the students who pick up from the tone and manner adopted by the teacher that it is all right to talk about the Advisor in this manner.

STILL IMAGE (DEMONSTRATED BY TEACHER AND READ BY STUDENTS)

After all the Bs have given their impressions of the Advisors, the teacher says, "Have you ever looked at a photo of someone who you can never meet, like a grandparent who is no longer living, or a picture of an historical figure, and made judgments about whether you would have liked each other if you had met? I do that sometimes. I look at a photo and say to myself, 'I like this person. He looks like he'd be fun, or interesting, or whatever.' When you do that you are *reading* the picture. You are picking up clues from the picture, using many clues to make a judgment. The way the person is sitting or standing, what the person is doing, the facial expression, the clothes — all these things give clues as to whether you'd like the person.

We can make pictures ourselves, using our own bodies. These are called *still images*. I am going to make a still image for you now and I'd like you to just have a look at it."

The teacher then poses sitting with a book, reading with an exasperated look. The teacher creates the image for the students, holds it for about a minute, relaxes and then says, "I'm sure you got many different impressions while looking at that image. I am going to make it again and this time I want you to call out any impressions you get from the image, so we'll know what everyone is seeing."

The teacher goes into still image again, while students call out their impressions. The impressions can be discussed, especially if there is a wide range of opinions as to what is being depicted. The teacher should also discuss the qualities of the still image.

The teacher's modeling of the still image provides a good example for the students. The most important feature is that the image be absolutely still, with the eyes focused, not blinking or moving. Demonstrate to the students the importance of what the eyes are focused on by presenting your still image again. Do not move anything and keep the eyes focused. If the eyes were originally on the book, a simple change of looking beyond the book changes the whole picture. Discuss with the students the expression on your face. What does it tell them? The body — what does it say?

Then ask the students to think about what the Advisors do when they aren't working? How do they spend their leisure time?

STUDENTS CREATE A STILL IMAGE ('READ' BY TEACHER)

The teacher then asks the students to create their own still image

68

showing the Advisors at their leisure. The still image should be like a candid photo taken of the Advisor when s/he is not expecting it. It should show what the Advisor is doing as well as reveal an attitude to the activity. Each student is to take a space in the room to create an image. The teacher will 'read' all the images when they have been created. Some time is given for this. Then the teacher tells the students that at the clap of hands, they are to freeze into their images and hold them while s/he 'reads' them. The teacher counts, 'One, two, three' and then claps hands, saying, 'Freeze.'

While the students are frozen, the teacher comments aloud on what she can see. For example, "I can see that many of the Advisors lead quite sedentary lives. They are readers and thinkers, and many spend their leisure time writing. However, some are very active, being engaged in archery and riding and even wrestling. They seem to be a fairly contented lot, so their lives must suit them." It is important to feed back to the students what you actually see. If many are unclear to you, you can indicate that by saying something like, "Many of them are engaged in pursuits which I don't understand, but I can tell by their expressions that they enjoy life."

Comment: Bear in mind that this part of the drama is difficult for students who have not done this kind of work before. Up until this time, they have had to commit only their thinking to the drama. Making a still image requires that they commit themselves bodily to the work. They are now engaged in both body and mind. For many, this is a difficult step.

Session two
IMAGING THE ROOM

Teacher: "I wonder what the room is like where the Advisors and Queen meet. Close your eyes and see if you can get an image of the Royal Meeting Room? How big is it compared to the room we are in? The same size? Twice as big? Half as big? How high are the ceilings? Are they straight across, arched, or vaulted? What colors are in the room? Where in the Palace is it? Is it at the top? Are there windows in the room? What are they like? What shape are they? How many windows are there? Walk to the window and look out. What do you see? What is the landscape like? Is it hilly? Flat? Are there mountains? Is it near the sea? Look around and see what kind of vegetation there is. What else can you see from the window? Come back into the room. Look around. What are the walls like? What are they made of? If I ran my hands over them, what would they feel like? Are they rough or smooth? Cold or warm to touch? Is there anything hanging on the walls? What? What is the floor like? What is it made of? What kind of furniture is in the room? If there is a meeting table, what shape is it? What is it made of? What kind of chairs are in the room? Is there anything else in this Royal Meeting Room? Open your eyes."

The teacher then says that obviously, with 30 people doing this imaging together, there are probably 30 different rooms in people's heads. Could each of them work with a partner and discuss their respective rooms?

DRAWING THE ROOM AND WRITING A DESCRIPTION

The teacher continues: "After you have done this, I would like you to work together to draw a room. To do this, you will need to describe your rooms to each other and see if you agree on anything. Then you'll have to come to some sort of compromise on what your room will look like. The drawing should help you sort out your impressions."

Comment: To do this task, the students must cooperate and negotiate with each other.

While the students talk and draw, the teacher circulates, asking questions which help the students clarify their ideas. When the drawings are completed, the students are asked to write a description of the room.

Comment: The drawing and talking are valuable prewriting activites. If the children are very young, the teacher can become a scribe, asking them to describe orally the room as she writes. The best time to do this is while they are drawing.

If the teacher does not want to spend time with writing and drawing here, s/he could just say, "We are going to go to that room together in a minute, so we must agree on one particular room. Here's what we'll do. Each person can give us one feature of the room and then we'll have a collective room which comes from everybody's imagination. So, could we agree that whatever information is offered will become a feature of the room and we'll accept that, even if it is different from our own personal images?"

The teacher then asks how big this room is. Whatever information is supplied by the students is accepted until a collective image of the room is created.

Session three
SETTING UP THE ROOM PHYSICALLY

The teacher asks, "Do you think you could create that room here, using just the furniture that we have at our disposal?"

She then stands back and allows the students to rearrange the furniture so that it can represent the Royal Meeting Room. Although this is generally a noisy procedure, it doesn't last long. It is also very useful to observe the young people solving this space problem without the teacher's help. If difficulties arise s/he can simply stop them and help sort things out. The most important thing for the students seems to be getting the shape of the meeting table right. Whether they have opted for a round table or a long rectangular one, it is best to check with them when it's ready by asking, "Is this how you want it? Is this the right shape?" Left to their own devices, most classes can sort this out without any intervention.

FINDING A WAY OF SITTING AND STANDING

While the students are still at their desks, the teacher asks them to experiment with different ways of sitting to make them feel more like adult Advisors. She asks them to freeze on a hand clap signal so they can make a still image to depict the Advisor in the Royal Meeting Room.

The teacher then asks the students to move away from the desks so that they can find a way of standing which makes them feel like adult Advisors. When they have found their positions, the teacher freezes them with a hand clap. While they are frozen in various attitudes, the teacher narrates.

STILL IMAGE WHILE TEACHER NARRATES

Teacher: "One morning, all the Advisors were informed that there

71

was an important meeting in the Royal Meeting Room. They were amazed because it was called for nine in the morning and they never met at such an early hour. As they dressed for the meeting they wondered what was the matter. Something terrible must have happened! There were rumors all over the Palace. The Ladies-in-Waiting were saying that the Queen had been up all night! Some said that she had been crying! All the Advisors were baffled. What had happened? They gathered outside the Meeting Room, talking in hushed voices. Something terrible was wrong, but what?''

SPEAKING THOUGHTS OUT LOUD

The teacher then tells the class: ''While the Royal Advisors were waiting, they were thinking of the many things that could have gone wrong. I'm going to come around and put my hand on some of your shoulders and if I do, I'd like you to tell us what that Advisor is thinking while waiting outside the Royal Meeting Room. I want to hear just the one thought that is in your head at the moment I put my hand on your shoulder.''

The teacher then circulates, placing a hand on some of the students' shoulders. The following responses were made by a Grade 4 class and are fairly typical of what is said by students at this stage of the drama.

> ''I don't know what's wrong.''
> ''Maybe the baby's sick.''
> ''I hope I can help her.''
> ''Maybe it's to do with the King.''
> ''I don't know what to think.''
> ''I'll be able to solve the problem, whatever it is.''
> ''I'm worried.''
> ''I'm nervous.''
> ''What's wrong with her?''

Comment: This technique, *speaking thoughts out loud*, enables the teacher to gauge how committed the students are to the drama. If the commitment and belief are there, then the students' thoughts will help set a mood for the meeting. If the students are at a loss for words or if they fall about giggling, then the teacher knows that they are not ready to go on with the drama.

If this happens, the teacher should back up, talk with the students and do more building-belief activities, such as talking, writing, and researching if necessary.

If 'speaking thoughts out loud' reveals that the students are committed to the drama, the teacher continues.

MEETING OF THE QUEEN AND HER ADVISORS

Teacher: "I am going to the door and when I come back I will try to behave and think like that young Queen, and I would like you to try to think like those Advisors."

The teacher goes to the door, pauses, and turns around, in role. Teacher, in role as the Queen: "Ladies and gentlemen, please come straight into the Meeting Room."

The Queen leads the way in and sits. The Advisors follow. The teacher, in role, announces: "Ladies and gentlemen, thank you for being so prompt. I realize that it is very early and I apologize for the inconvenience. I would not have convened the meeting if it were not an urgent matter. The fact is . . . well, I suppose I will just have to tell you straight out what the problem is.

"Some time ago, before I became your Queen, a young man named Jack Simpson did me a great favor. I am not going to tell you what it was, for, quite frankly, it is none of your business. However, he did this favor for me and in return I promised him something. I promised him that I would give him my first-born child when I had one. Now, I didn't realize what I was saying. I mean, I didn't even know if I would have a baby or not and, well, you know that I have recently given birth to a beautiful baby daughter, and, well . . . Mr. Simpson has come for her. He came last night and said that he had come to claim her, just as I had promised. Only now I realize that I don't want to give her up. I need your help with this problem. What shall I do?"

Comment: *Wait Time* The teacher, in role as Queen, must now wait for the students, in role as Advisors, to respond. The key here is to keep quiet and simply wait. This is difficult for many teachers to do. When I began this way of working I found it difficult to keep quiet, so I used a technique which I learned from Mary Budd Rowe, a science educator, who advised me to simply count silently how many seconds I was planning to wait after I had posed a question. I discovered that three seconds seems a very long time in a classroom if no one speaks. Ten seconds is an eternity. However, I soon discovered that the kind of response one gets after ten seconds of silence is invariably much more thoughtful than one which happens immediately. Thinking takes time. The kind of questions posed in role drama require thought, and students must be given time to reflect so that their answers will be thoughtful.

The question which the teacher, in role as Queen, has posed to these Advisors has no simple answer. It is a good idea to count up to 20 after asking the Advisors what to do, before speaking again. Once the students realize that you will wait, they will begin thinking seriously.

Very often students know that, normally, the teacher will ask them questions to which she knows the answer, wait about two seconds for an answer, and then give the answer. These are 'teacher type' questions and we've all asked and answered them in our teaching careers. It wasn't until I began this kind of drama work that I realized that asking questions to which I already knew the answer does not encourage thinking. What it does encourage is a sort of guessing game where the students try to guess at the answer that is in the teacher's head.

In this role drama, when the young Queen says, "I don't know what to do," she really doesn't. In role drama, students realize very quickly that the questions posed are real. The teacher doesn't know the answer and cannot supply one.

THE SCRIPT

When the teacher first goes into role with the class, it is important to provide all the information the students will need to go on with the drama. The teacher must indicate, through the way she behaves, the tone of voice, and what she says, who the character is; what the problem is; who the students are and what is expected from them. What the teacher says at the beginning of the meeting must be specific and helpful.

The first time you do a role drama, write down what you need to convey at the beginning. For "The Story of Jack Simpson," I created a monologue, a piece of script that included everything I thought the Advisors needed to know. I practised the script and rehearsed before I went into role with the students so that when I became the young Queen, it would work. Never underestimate the power of rehearsal. It is invaluable.

An important thing to keep in mind when going into role and when writing a script is to be low key. Do not enter in a 'dramatic' way with large gestures and stage delivery. This will most certainly cause embarrassment among the students, resulting in laughter or an attempt to match your theatrical display. This can only lead to phoney theatrics rather than a group trying to think like Advisors. When the Queen delivers her monologue to her Advisors, she does so with dignity and respect for them. Clearly she signals by her behavior and her words that she respects them and is relying on their judgment. She is also controlled, although clearly upset. You may wish, in fact, to use a real-life statesperson as your model. When I go into this role, I use Queen Elizabeth as my model and try to think and behave as I believe she would in these circumstances. It works for me. I also think in terms of a TV performance rather than one for the stage, and that also helps.

PLANNING

So far, the teacher has been able to plan the drama, deciding what story will be used and what building-belief strategies will be employed to advance the drama. However, once the crucial question is posed, "What will I do?", the teacher signals to the students that they now have the power to take over the drama. It is up to them to decide. Now the teacher and the class are in unknown waters. No one knows where they are going. However, both students and teacher know what their purpose is. They must find a solution to a serious problem. The teacher, in role, must now listen carefully and respond fairly to what is said, always keeping in mind that her response must be as the Queen.

A description of what happened in a Grade 6 class follows. The students are in role as Advisors.

S1: Why don't you run away? Take the baby and run.
T: Where would I run to?
S1: Um, to another country.
T: Another kingdom?
S1: Yes.

T: How long would I have to stay away?
S1: What?

Comment: It is apparent that this student is surprised to be engaged in dialogue this way. He has already had a few minutes of the teacher's time and expects that it will now be someone else's turn. This is a common feature of some classrooms and usually means that as soon as a student has been pushed in his/her thinking, s/he is 'let off the hook'. This often means that the thinking goes no further.

T: I'm wondering how long I'd have to stay away.
S1: Well, till he goes away.
T: But he lives here, in this kingdom.
S1: He does?
T: Yes. So would that mean I must stay away forever?
S1: I guess so.
T: I don't want to do that. This is my home. I like it here.
S2: Why don't you give him another baby?
T: Another baby?
S2: Yes. Hide Princess Patricia and give him another baby.
T: Where would I get it?
S3: An orphanage.
S4: Yes.
T: But he's seen Princess Patricia.
S4: That doesn't matter.
T: But it does. He's seen her and he isn't stupid. He'd know. Besides, he lives in this kingdom. If I give him a baby and pretend it is Princess Patricia, I'll have to tell the whole kingdom that I've given her away. People will have to know. She's not just any baby. You can't keep secrets about the Royal Baby.
S5: That's right. I think you should give her to him.
T: But why? I don't want to.
S6: You made a promise.
T: But I didn't realize what I was saying.
S7: Why don't you just throw him in the dungeons? You're the Queen.
T: Yes. I've thought of that. I mean, I do have soldiers and guards. The only problem is, has he done anything wrong?
(Silence. The boy who suggested this looks very uncertain and shrugs. Again, a reflective silence. The Queen shrugs uncertainly.)

T: It is a question. Well?
S7: I don't know.

Comment: As can be seen from these exchanges, the teacher, in role, pushes the students deeper in their thinking by constantly opening up the implications of what they suggest. This is what creates a 'thinking climate' in the room. The teacher refuses to allow them to go for simple solutions and discourages glib and facile answers by challenging them to think further. The teacher behaves, in fact, like a young Queen with a serious problem, who has a group of Advisors whose job is to advise her.

The Advisors continue their discussion, suggesting among other things:

"Talk with him and see if he will take something else."

"Talk with him and explain that you didn't know what you were saying."

"Guard the baby and don't let him near it."

"Just say no. After all you are the Queen."

"Let the King handle it for you." (To this the Queen answers that the King is away on a hunting trip. He won't be back for ten days. She expresses fear of what he will say when he finds out that she promised their firstborn child to someone she hardly knew.)

Comment: The teacher does this, because having someone else handle the dilemma is an abdication of the group's responsibility. They are the ones who have all the knowledge; indeed, it is their job to advise her. She does not allow them to fob off the responsibility to someone who isn't there.

"Throw him in the dungeons anyway. It's not really right to do that, but you have no choice."

"Give him the baby because you promised him, and promises should be kept."

"Talk to him and see if you can find out why he wants the baby."

"Share the baby in some way."

During the discussion the Queen admits that she doesn't know very much about this man at all other than that he seems to live in the kingdom and knows things, and he did her a great favor which was important to her. He is not stupid; in fact, he is a very powerful man. However, she does not know why he wants the baby, where he lives exactly, or who he is.

After 20 minutes of discussion that results in little agreement as to what should be done, the Queen can say, "Ladies and gentlemen, I'm grateful for all your suggestions, but I am still confused as to what I should do. There have been so many suggestions, I hardly know which one to take. Perhaps if they were put in writing, I would be able to read them carefully and make some firm decisions. I am therefore asking that you retire to your respective chambers and put your thoughts in writing. When I have your suggestions on paper, I will meet with you again. I would like that to be this afternoon, as there is urgency here. Jack Simpson has given me only three days and today is already half over. Thank you." Then she departs.

Comment: The writing was not part of the teacher's preplanning but something she decided to do because there was no clear direction from the Advisors. If the Advisors had been able to come to some kind of consensus, she would have simply followed their advice. Writing is an excellent way to crystalize thought. At this point in the role drama, then, the teacher, in role as Queen, hopes that the writing will help to clarify the situation.

WRITING IN ROLE AS ADVISORS

The teacher steps out of role as Queen and organizes papers, pens, and desks so that the students can write alone. The students write their advice.

CLASSIFYING THE WRITTEN RESPONSES

When everyone has written, the teacher gathers the students around and tells them that she is going to classify the ideas she has received in writing. The first one is read out. It advises that the Queen get out the guards and stop Jack from entering the Palace. The teacher says, "I am going to classify this one under the heading 'Use violence'. So anything to do with guards or soldiers or threats or killing I'll put there. All right?"

Then the teacher asks one student to take all the suggestions in the 'violence' classification and gives the student the first paper.

The next letter suggests talking to Jack to see if something can be worked out. The teacher gives this to another student who agrees to hold all the responses classified 'talk'.

As each is read, the students and teacher together decide on classifications for the letters. When all were read and tabulated, the following information emerged:

CLASSIFICATION	NUMBER OF RESPONSES
Violence (Kill him; call out the guards.)	2
Running away (Go to another kingdom; to your father's place; for a holiday; hide in Palace.)	6
Trickery (Get a baby from an orphanage; substitute a doll for baby; tell him you'll give him the baby and then say she's sick; say she died.)	7
Abdicating responsibility (Let the King handle it.)	1
Stall him (Arrange other meetings; say you need more time; offer other things.)	4
Talk with Jack (See if you can find out why he wants the baby; negotiate; appeal to his compassion.)	10

REFLECTING ON THE DRAMA

The students and the teacher discuss what has happened so far. They talk about the implications of each category of suggestions.

Session four
DISCUSSING AND PLANNING

The teacher asks the students what they would like to do next. Unanimously they decide to meet with Jack.

The teacher asks, "Would you like me to play Jack?"

The students endorse this idea with enthusiasm.

The teacher then asks who will play the Queen. There are several volunteers, including two boys. This is greeted with laughter by the class. The teacher does not laugh, but asks the boy nearest her, "Do you think you could play this important role seriously? It will mean that you will have to think like a woman, which could be hard because you are male." The boy says he thinks he could. The teacher explains that there is no reason why boys can't play girls' roles and vice versa. She points out that she will be playing a man when she is Jack Simpson, and the group recognized that. The group agrees. The boy is to play the Queen.

Then the teacher asks, "Why do we want to meet with Jack?"

Comment: At this stage, the role drama is being planned as it occurs. The students decide that they want to talk with Jack, which opens a potentially new learning area. The drama can now be about how you judge another person's character or how can you negotiate with a stranger.

Sometimes the students may want a class member to be Jack. If this happens, the teacher must support the class wish and then help the student who is playing Jack to think about who he is, why he wants the baby, and whether he is willing to negotiate. The teacher would then remain in role as Queen and from that position be able to pose questions which push the group in their thinking. She could also play devil's advocate and inject the necessary surprise and tension which is needed to keep the drama moving.

DISCUSSING STRATEGIES FOR NEGOTIATING WITH JACK

A discussion ensues in which it becomes apparent that some students are simply curious about Jack Simpson, while others want to judge whether he is the type of person who could care for a child properly. A large group wants to see if they can talk him out of taking the baby.

The teacher suggests that the class divide into groups to talk over what they think they want to say to him. The groups form and talk. During this discussion period, the teacher circulates, joining in to help and posing questions to encourage thinking.

Some students seem to have forgotten how powerful Jack is and they are making plans to capture him.

MAKING A LIST OF WHAT WE KNOW AND FEEL

The teacher decides that it would be useful for the class to articulate collectively both what they know about Jack and what they intuit. On the board, the teacher sets up two columns and asks the class to suggest what should go in them. The result follows:

ABOUT JACK SIMPSON
This we know:
> He wants the baby.
> He knows where things are in the Palace.
> He comes and goes as he pleases.
> He is male.
> He did the Queen a great favor.
> He's powerful.
> He said he'd wait three days for the baby.
> He said he was a reasonable man.

This we feel:
> He may have magical powers.
> He is to be trusted.
> He is reasonable.
> He's sneaky.
> He will probably take something else instead of the baby.
> We should be nice to him because he may do something terrible to us or to the Queen.
> We should treat him firmly, but be nice.
> He is asking too much from the Queen.

While the students compile these lists, an animated discussion occurs. Although there is firm agreement on what the facts are regarding Jack, there is much disagreement about how people feel about him. Most of the students, however, do see him as a reasonable type of person and they are confident that they can 'make him see reason.'

CLASS DISCUSSING DIFFERENCES BETWEEN FACT AND FEELING

Both teacher and students talk about the differences between facts

81

and feelings, and about when one's feelings should be trusted and taken into consideration when making decisions.

Because the teacher knows that the students are expecting Jack to be reasonable and 'nice,' she realizes that when she goes into role as Jack, she must surprise them and create some tension in order to sustain their involvement. Very quickly the teacher must decide why Jack wants the baby and whether he can be negotiated with.

Comment: If the teacher is inexperienced with role drama, she may stop the session here so that there is time to prepare more. The drama can be stopped at almost any point and picked up again hours or even days later. This is never a problem. If the students are interested in the drama, they will readily focus themselves again into role and into the situation. If they aren't interested, the drama should be dropped.

SETTING UP THE ROOM PHYSICALLY

The room is set up again into the Royal Meeting Room as before. The teacher insists that all superfluous things be removed from the area, such as school books, pencil cases, and bags. The area should look as much as possible like the picture they have in their minds, and they shouldn't let the school environment encroach upon it.

REHEARSAL

The teacher asks the class whether they feel they can treat the boy playing the Queen as if he were their Queen. She points out that they may need to practise this and asks for suggestions as to how the Queen should be addressed. After some discussion they agree that the Queen will be addressed as "Your Majesty."

The teacher asks whether they want to begin the meeting before Jack comes in, at the moment he comes in, or after he comes in. They decide on 'at the moment Jack comes in.'

STOP-FRAME TECHNIQUE

The teacher explains *stop-frame technique*, telling the students that it is like stopping a video while it is playing so that the action freezes. (This technique has been used in Grade 3 and up. It may be too difficult for younger children.) The teacher explains that she will come into the room as Jack and just before Jack sits she will say, "Stop frame." On this signal, both Jack and the Advisors will freeze. Then the Advisor sitting on Jack's immediate right will speak aloud what he or she is thinking at the moment Jack appears. The teacher explains that this is difficult work, and that she is willing to wait to hear what people are thinking, and the group will remain frozen throughout. When all the Advisors have spoken in turn, Jack will say what is on his mind and the meeting will begin. They do this. Among the thoughts are:

"He looks okay to me."
"I wonder where he lives."
"I wonder why he wants the baby."
"He seems reasonable."
"He looks very ordinary."
"I don't trust him."

The teacher, in role as Jack, says, "I hope this meeting won't take long. I'm in a hurry."

Comment: The teacher deliberately injects the tension of time into the drama. As well, she refrains from telling the group too much. She wants the students to speculate.

THE MEETING OF JACK, THE ADVISORS, AND THE QUEEN

Jack says, "Well, Your Majesty, I've come to this meeting as I promised. (To the Advisors) Now, what can I do for you?"

The Advisors try to find out what they can about Jack, who is quite evasive. He does not look people in the eye when they speak to him, and although he smiles and speaks quietly, he is reluctant to tell them much about himself or his background. When one of the Advisors asks him point blank what he intends to do with the baby, he pauses for a long time. Then —

Jack: Must I answer that, Your Majesty?
Queen: They want to know.
Jack: (Pauses, looks at floor, then directly at the Advisors.) I want to teach it things.
Adv. 1: What kinds of things?

Jack: (pauses) Magic.

There is a murmur of interest from the Advisors. Obviously some find this exciting and interesting; others appear to have misgivings.

Adv 2: Isn't she a little young to teach things to?

Jack: No, sir. I need to have them very young for this kind of teaching.

Adv 3: Exactly what kind of teaching is it?

Jack: Do you mean what kinds of things do I do?

Adv 3: Yes.

Jack: I'm afraid I cannot tell you that.

Adv 4: Will this magic you teach her be good magic or bad magic?

Jack: (smiles) There is no difference.

Jack's statement creates obvious tension. Some Advisors who were quite happy for the baby to be taught magic are now looking doubtful.

The Advisors try to talk Jack out of taking the baby. Jack is polite but insistent. He reminds them that the Queen promised him the baby. He asks the Queen to tell the Advisors that this is true. The Queen supports this, admitting that she did promise, and that he once did a very great favor for her. One of the Advisors suggests that Jack could come and live in the Palace and do his teaching there. Jack says he is very interested in this idea. He asks, "Could I have the Royal Princess alone for five hours every day?" The Advisors aren't sure about this. Jack explains that he needs this much time in order to teach her. After some discussion, the Advisors agree and Jack leaves to collect his things so that he can move in. The drama ends.

Session five
REFLECTING ON THE DRAMA

The teacher and the students discuss the drama. The teacher asks them if they are satisfied with the ending. Some students feel uneasy about Jack and do not like his demand to have the baby alone for five hours a day. The teacher points out that schools have children for five hours a day to teach them. The students reflect on this. One student suggests that you have to be careful who you let teach your children. The teacher agrees. There is some discussion on the importance of teachers. There is also discussion about the issue of promises and whether they should be kept. Many students do not believe that promises should always be kept. They give examples of times when adults and children do not keep promises. Some students feel that promises are important, but they believe that this promise was a hard one to keep. One student, suggesting that people should think before they promise, says that the young Queen made a promise without thinking about the consequences. They talk about what the King will say when he returns, and also of what might happen ten years from now.

Much speculation centres on what the baby will be like years later and whether she will use her magical powers well.

WRITING A REPORT TO THE KING

The teacher suggests that the King would want a full report on Jack Simpson when he returns. After all, Jack is a stranger. He will want to know why the Advisors made this decision and what their opinion is of Jack's character. The students write their reports. Some examples follow:

Your Majesty the King:

As you already know, the Queen has appointed Jack Simpson to be the Royal Protector of Princess Patricia. I myself fully agree with the Queen. The Queen said she promised Jack Simpson her baby, and I think promises should be kept depending on the situation. In this situation, I don't think the promise should be kept.

Mr. Simpson accepted our proposal that he come and live in the Palace and will start work tomorrow. We all hope that you will not be too mad, but it has to be this way or you may never see your daughter again.

Sincerely,
Your Royal Advisor,
Stephanie

Your Majesty the King:

As your Advisor, I would like to comment about the situation between Her Majesty the Queen and Mr. Jack Simpson. I think Mr. Simpson should forget about the promise of taking Princess Patricia. Well, I don't really agree with the Queen for letting Mr. Simpson teach Patricia magic, but I guess it is the only reasonable answer to the problem.

Now, about this Jack Simpson, he seems to have a short temper and is very "closed up" about his past. Just the other day, one of the Royal Advisors asked him about his past and he snapped at her. Mr. Simpson says he knows magic and has special powers.

And last of all, I would like to comment on my opinion on promises. I agree that the promise made by the Queen was not very bright but she was young and she said that what Mr. Simpson did for her was very important. She said that it was a matter of life and death.

I have given you the facts and when you arrive at the castle you will get the small details from the Queen.

Yours sincerely,
Your Royal Advisor,
Jyotika

Writing and role drama

Writing in role is a very powerful building-belief strategy, as it requires students to commit their thoughts to paper while they think in the context of the drama. Conversely, the drama acts as a powerful stimulus for writing, creating a meaningful context. Writing in role has a specific purpose and an audience that is defined by the drama situation. Students readily pick up pens and write freely. Often the quantity and quality of the writing is far superior to writing done in other school contexts. The drama also provides opportunities for students to write in a variety of styles and forms. In the set of role drama lessons described above, the students wrote only twice, but there were other opportunities for writing if the teacher had wished to use them.

- Writing an autobiography in role. This could be done after the pair interviewing. (See Session One.)
- Writing a newspaper profile of an Advisor. This could also be done after the pair interviewing.
- Writing a diary entry after the first meeting with the Queen.

- Writing a diary entry after Jack agrees to stay.
- Writing a letter to a friend a year after Jack has been in the Palace, telling what things are happening that involve Princess Patricia.
- Writing as Princess Patricia when she is 12.
- Writing one's memoirs as an old Advisor, 20 years later.
- Writing a diary entry, in role as the Queen, on the evening before her husband, the King, returns.
- Writing a letter from the Queen to her daughter, to be opened on Princess Patricia's eighteenth birthday, that explains the whole story of how Jack came to be her tutor.
- Writing a newspaper report on the hiring of Jack Simpson as Royal Tutor.

Role drama across the curriculum

Within the context of the drama, opportunities arise for art, social studies, and other curriculum activities. As part of their experience in this role drama, the students may:

- research life in castles so that they learn about medieval times
- draw their own quarters in the Palace
- draw a floor plan of the castle
- create a mural of the castle and its environs
- research which people are employed in advisory roles in modern society.

Selected references

Rumplestiltskin. Retold and illustrated by Paul Galdone. New York: Clarion Books, 1985.

Rumplestiltskin. Retold by Dorothy Joan Harris and illustrated by Regolo Ricci. Toronto: Oxford University Press, 1991.

Rumplestiltskin. Retold by Alison Sage and illustrated by Gennady Spirin. London: A. and C. Black, 1991.

Rumplestiltskin. Retold and illustrated by Paul O. Zelinsky. New York: E.P. Dutton/Toronto: Fitzhenry & Whiteside, 1986.

5

....

Folktale source — "The Pied Piper"

In this chapter, a role drama based on the story of the Pied Piper is described in detail. "The Pied Piper" is an excellent source for drama for the following reasons:

A number of groups take part in the story, and their problems can form the basis for drama — the Councillors, the townspeople, the children, and even the rats!

A number of issues can become the focus for the drama, for example:

- How can the rat problem be solved?
- How can the Councillors make amends for not honoring the contract?
- How can the children survive in the new land?

Students take on the roles of both Councillors and townspeople, grappling with the problem of what can be done about the children's disappearance.

Time frame and grade level

The drama described in the following pages was carried out in five sessions of approximately one and a half hours each (approximately eight hours of work altogether). However, the same drama can be expanded to a twelve-hour period, or condensed into three hours.

The description that follows is of a Grade 5 class at work. The drama has also been done successfully with Grades 4, 6, 7, and 8, as well as with adult teachers. It works with all age levels.

Teaching strategies

The following outline shows the teacher's planning for this role drama.

SESSION ONE

> Telling the story
> Posing a question to wonder about
> Compiling a list
> Writing a letter in role

SESSION TWO

> Posing a question
> Students think while teacher questions
> Talking in pairs
> Drawing a collective mural of the Town of Hamelin
> Teacher in role as a stranger

SESSION THREE

> Moving back in time — the election promise
> Setting up the room physically
> Establishing a symbol for the meeting
> Still image
> The meeting (whole-group drama with teacher in role as Mayor, students in role as Councillors)
> Reflecting

SESSION FOUR

> Writing town cries and designing posters

SESSION FIVE

> Planning the next stage of the drama (large group)
> Planning in small groups

Setting up the room physically
Sharing the power
Stop-frame technique
The meeting with the Piper
Writing in role
Reflections

Session one
TELLING THE STORY

The Story of the Pied Piper

Once there was a town called Hamelin. And the people of Hamelin had a terrible problem. Their problem was *rats*!

Rats, rats, rats,
They fought the dogs and killed the cats
And bit the babies in their cradles
And ate the cheeses out of the vats
And licked the soup from the cooks' own ladles,
Split open the kegs of salted sprats,
Made nests inside men's Sunday hats
And even spoiled the women's chats
By drowning their speaking with shrieking and squeaking
In fifty different sharps and flats!
(from Robert Browning's poem)

Now, it wasn't funny. Living with rats is certainly not pleasant. I don't know how much you know about rats, but they are very nasty. For a start, they carry all kinds of terrible diseases, and if they bite you, you can get very sick. Just imagine what it was like. Whenever the people of Hamelin opened their food cupboards, say to get something for breakfast, there were already rats in there eating their food! Mothers, when they put their babies to sleep, had to check all the bedclothes to make sure that no rats were lurking there. It was horrible!

Finally the people of Hamelin got so fed up they stormed off to the Town Hall to complain to the Mayor and Councillors who were meeting there. They just marched right into the Council chambers and addressed the meeting, saying, "We are absolutely fed up with this rat situation. We elected you people to our Town Council to deal with situations like this. That's your job. We want some action and *now!*"

The Mayor, who was looking rather pale (he wasn't used to

townspeople storming into his meeting), said, "We're doing all we can. We've struck committees and called in experts. We know how desperate the situation is. Don't forget, we live in this town too. Please, we are doing our very best."

But the people were angry and their spokesperson replied, "Your best is not good enough. We want something done now, and if it isn't, then you can say goodbye to your cushy jobs, because we are going to vote you out of office!"

And so saying, they stormed out, leaving the Mayor and Councillors very upset, for it was true, they had done their best and could think of nothing else to do. So they sat in gloomy silence, thinking about how their jobs would be lost, when suddenly there was a gentle tap tap on the door of the Council chamber.

"Oh, what's that?" cried the Mayor. "Is it a rat?"

"Oh, don't be silly, Mayor. It is just someone at the door," assured a Councillor.

"Oh," said the Mayor, collecting himself, "of course. Come in."

Through the door came a strange figure. He was very tall and very thin, with strange, bright eyes as sharp as pins. He seemed to be both smiling and not smiling at the same time. Later, people said of him that he had lips "where smiles went out and in." He wore his hair long, which was very unusual, and his dress was most peculiar. Instead of wearing a suit and tie like the Councillors, he was wearing a robe, half of which was red, the other half, yellow. Around his waist was a silken cord and attached to it was a silver flute. He seemed very strange.

"Who are you?" demanded the Mayor.

The young man bowed. "I am called the Pied Piper. I believe that you have a small problem with rats, is that right?"

"A *small* problem?" bellowed the Mayor. "A *giant* problem!"

"Well, I can fix it for you," said the Pied Piper.

The Mayor looked at him in disbelief. "You? How could a strange fellow like you solve our rat problem?" And he laughed.

"It is my secret how, and I will do it for you, if you agree to pay me one thousand guilders." (Guilders were the kind of money they had in Hamelin.)

"One thousand?" the Mayor fairly screamed. "If you can solve our rat problem, we'd give you fifty thousand. Right, Councillors?"

The Councillors thumped the table in agreement.

"No," said the Piper, "one thousand guilders is quite enough. If I rid Hamelin of rats, will you agree to pay me one thousand guilders?"

"Of course," replied the Mayor, and the Piper shook hands with the Mayor and all the Councillors as well. The bargain was struck.

(At this point the teacher would shake hands with as many of the students as possible, saying to each. "Is it agreed?" This symbolic gesture will be important later in the drama.)

The Piper stepped into the square outside the Town Hall. Now, in many European cities there is a town square where people can gather. Hamelin had a square like that. It was all cobblestones, with a fountain in the middle. All the important buildings, like the Town Hall, faced onto it. The Piper walked to the middle of the square, and placing his flute to his lips, he began to play. His music was so sweet, all the passers-by stopped and listened. As they listened, there was a scratching sound which got louder and louder until it became a great rumbling and then out of the houses the rats came tumbling! Grey rats, white rats, tawny rats, scrawny rats. Brown rats, black rats, old rats, young rats. All kinds of rats were squeaking and swirling around the feet of the Pied Piper.

The people were appalled — ugh, they didn't want to be near those rats, so they drew back to the edges of the square and watched in amazement as the Piper, still playing his flute, left the square and made his way along the twisted, narrow cobblestone streets of Hamelin. And the rats followed. The people followed too, but at a discreet distance, watching as the Piper came to the edge of the town. Here there was a fast flowing river called the Weser, and while the Hamelin people watched, the Piper stood on the edge of the river, calmly playing his pipe as the rats tumbled past him into the river and were drowned!

You should have heard the Hamelin people! They rang the church bells until they rocked the steeple! Everyone was so happy that the rats were gone. The Mayor wandered around shaking hands.

(Teacher should shake more hands here.)

"Vote for me again. I told you we'd clear this problem up. Remember to vote for us next time."

Suddenly, in the middle of this general rejoicing the Pied Piper appeared, saying, "If you please, sir, my thousand guilders."

"Thousand guilders?" replied the Mayor, looking somewhat puzzled, "What thousand guilders?"

The Piper was not amused. "The thousand guilders you promised to pay me when I rid the town of the rats. I've done that. Now I would like to be paid."

The Mayor looked very vague. "Come now, a thousand guilders is a little expensive and I'm sure I wouldn't have agreed to that. I certainly don't remember it, do you, Councillors?" The Councillors shook their heads and looked vague also.

"Don't trifle with me" was the Piper's angry reply. "Folks who put me in a passion find I pipe to a different fashion."

The Mayor looked black. "Are you threatening me, sir? I am the Mayor of this town and do not take kindly to those who threaten me. I'd be happy to give you a few guilders and provide you with an expensive meal and some good wine. Take it or leave it." And so saying he turned on his heel and went off to dinner with his companions.

Once more the Piper stepped into the street. Again he put his flute to his lips and again he played such sweet music, it made people stop and listen. As he played there were faint sounds of hands clapping, then feet tapping and fingers clicking, and a rustling that turned to a bustling, and suddenly, out of the houses, the children of Hamelin came running. All the Hamelin children who could walk or run were suddenly swirling around the Piper, just like the rats. The townspeople felt bewitched and could not stop their children, but only follow as the Piper once more made his way through the narrow twisted streets of Hamelin. In horror, they watched as he headed for the rushing waters of the river Weser. Surely he wasn't going to drown their children.

But no, to their relief, they saw him turn away from the river. Now, outside of Hamelin there was a large mountain, and there was no road over it and no road around it and when the townspeople saw the Piper heading for it, they were very relieved because they knew that he could not get around or over it and they thought that he would stop and their children would come back. But no. They watched in astonishment as a great door suddenly appeared in the mountainside. The Piper entered. The children followed. The door closed, then disappeared. The children were gone forever.

Comment: I always wait in silence at the end of this story, letting the students think about it. Very often a student says, "Is that a true story?" I reply, "Not really. It comes from a long narrative poem written by Robert Browning. However, the town of Hamelin does exist in Germany and apparently it is an old story from there. Many people think it has some truth to it."

In fact, there is some very interesting speculation as to the origin of the story. One theory is that it was a story told to explain the great plague which, of course, was spread by rats. The Piper is a personification of Death, who took the lives of many children. In Browning's poem, the children went to a perfect land where they were happy forever — Heaven.

Another theory is that during the Middle Ages in Europe, when child labor was the order of the day, men often came recruiting children for work in other parts of Europe. Those children were often never seen again. The story may be an attempt to explain that.

This information is best withheld from the students at this point, so that they will wonder and think for themselves.

POSING A QUESTION TO WONDER ABOUT

The teacher begins by saying: "It's an interesting story which always makes me think. The thing that I wonder about most is what effect the children's leaving had on the town of Hamelin. It has implications for everybody, not just the parents and relatives, but for the whole town.

It might be interesting if we made a list on the board of all the people who might have been affected by the children's disappearance. Who will we write down?"

Comment: The teacher invites the students to make a list. This intellectual task is relatively easy for students beyond the primary grades. Having them think along these lines begins to open up the implications of the children's disappearance. The thinking that they will do to make this list is the beginning of building commitment and belief in the drama. The students are already 'hooked into' the drama, even though they have not yet done anything which they would associate with drama. Making a list challenges the students to think more deeply about the story. A general rule to apply when working across the grades is: the more mature the students, the more intellectual the initial approach.

This ensures that more mature students are not faced with having to do anything at the beginning which makes them 'feel silly.' Gain their commitment bit by bit. This often means working slowly in the initial stages, especially if this way of working is unfamiliar to the students.

94

The teacher compiles the list on the board from the students' ideas. The following is a typical list offered by one Grade 5 class.

PEOPLE WHO MIGHT BE AFFECTED BY THE CHILDREN'S DISAPPEARANCE:

- parents and relatives
- school teachers
- school janitors, secretaries
- School Board people
- candy store owners and store clerks
- children's clothing store owners and store clerks
- manufacturers of children's toys, clothes and candy
- pediatricians (word supplied by teacher after children had offered 'children's doctors')
- writers of children's books
- entertainers of children — jugglers, clowns, puppeteers

WRITING A LETTER IN ROLE

The teacher asks the students to put themselves into one of the above-mentioned roles and try to think like that person. Their task is to compose a letter to the Mayor and Council which would be written a month after the children have disappeared. Their letter should tell the Mayor and Council just how they feel about their actions, informing them how the children's disappearance is affecting them personally.

Comment: The students are being asked to write a business letter. If one of the teacher's curriculum objectives is to teach the students this form of writing, then quite a lot of time could be spent here.

   In this kind of drama, writing happens spontaneously as part of the drama. The teacher can choose whether to make the writing a focus for a time, and delay the drama, or whether to use the writing primarily to generate ideas or clarify the moment in the drama. Sometimes there is justification for 'getting it right,' which entails time. A case can be made here, for example, to do the letters properly if we want the Council to take them seriously. If this is the case, time should be spent learning the correct form. Whatever is decided, the teacher should always provide an example of the kind of writing called for, since students are sometimes asked to write in forms they have never seen. A sample letter is shown to the group while the teacher briefly discusses how business letters differ from friendly letters.

Hamelin Elementary School
15 Weser Place
Hamelin
October 5th, 1886

The Mayor
Hamelin Town Council
Van Pelt Ave.
Hamelin

Mr. Mayor and Council:
I am writing on behalf of the Teachers' Association of Hamelin.
As you know, we are currently all unemployed as the children have been gone for over a month. We had hoped that they would have been returned by now, but as each day passes we lose hope of that happening.
The Teacher's' Unemployment Fund has now run out, and we are without work or funds. Our situation is getting desperate.
You created this problem by not honoring your contract with the Piper, so we want to know what you intend to do about our plight.
An early reply would be appreciated.
Yours faithfully,

Maria Van Hausen
President, Hamelin Teachers' Association.

The teacher points out that the name and address of the person to whom the letter is written appears below the writer's address on the left-hand side. The teacher also draws attention to the closure of a business letter. S/he then reads them a prepared sample letter.

The students then write their own letters. It is good practice for the teacher to write as well, assuming the same task as the students. Writing with them helps to gauge how long the task should take and provides a model for the students of 'writing behavior.'

Comment: A place in a corner of the room can be established where those who have finished writing first can gather with the teacher. Here they can circulate their letters and silently read each other's work. This keeps the students purposefully occupied. Not only are they reading, but they are getting an idea of the feelings in the town, all of which helps build belief and commitment to the drama.

Sometimes an additional task might be set for those who finish early. After they have read each other's letters, they may analyze the kinds of emotions that are evident in the letters. This is a higher level reading task involving inferencing and judging emotional tone of writing.

Session two
POSING A QUESTION

When all the letters have been written and most of them have been read, the teacher says, "I think it would be very interesting to find out how the Mayor and Councillors reacted when they received these letters."

S/he then explains that they can find out by working in role. The teacher agrees to take on the role of the Mayor and try to think like him, if the students will agree to take on the roles of Councillors and think like them. The teacher makes a contract with the students. They agree. (See chapter 4, pages 61-62, for an explanation of the type of language used in making such a contract with students.)

The teacher says: "If you are to take on the roles of the Town Councillors of Hamelin, you will need to think carefully before you begin. Decide specifically how old you are and how long you've been on the Council. What were your reasons for running for Council? Are you ambitious? Do you have any other jobs, other than being a Councillor? Are you a business man or woman? Or do you have some profession? Perhaps you are a lawyer or a doctor or a teacher. Are you married? Did you have children who were led away by the Piper? If so, you are probably going to feel very differently from a Councillor who doesn't have children. Where do you live in Hamelin? Could you describe your house to someone else so that that person could recognize it in a picture? How big is it? Is it made of stone or wood? Is there a garden? How old is it? When you walk through the front door, what things do you see? Exactly where is your house in the town of Hamelin? Is it near the square? Or is it nearer the River Weser? Who are your neighbors? How do you get on with them? What do you think they say about you to other people?"

Any questions which encourage the students to think about their roles and their life in the town of Hamelin are suitable, indeed, necessary.

TALKING IN PAIRS

Have the students discuss with a partner what they have decided about themselves as Councillors. They are to tell each other what things they have decided for their role. (They could interview each other instead, as was described in chapter 4, pages 64-65.)

DRAWING A COLLECTIVE MURAL OF THE TOWN OF HAMELIN

A large role of white newsprint is rolled diagonally across the classroom. The students together plan where the town square of Hamelin is, and then, working from one side of the newsprint, each student draws his/her own house in Hamelin.

TEACHER IN ROLE AS A STRANGER

While the students are working on the mural, the teacher

questions them about the town. S/he takes on the role of one who seeks information, asking such questions as (to the student drawing the church), "It looks very old, this church. When were the stained glass windows done? Are the people of this town very religious?" (To another student), "Could you recommend a reasonable place to stay in the town? What kind of food is served in the dining room?" (To another), "Is this town a good place to live? What does it have to recommend it?" The questions are designed to elicit detailed thinking about the town. They encourage the children to speculate. The more background the students have and the more thinking they do, the stronger will be their belief and commitment to the drama. The completed mural is displayed on the wall for the duration of the drama.

Session three
MOVING BACK IN TIME — THE ELECTION PROMISE

The teacher asks the students to move back in time to the year before the rats came to Hamelin. She asks them to remember why they decided to run for Council. What election promises did they make? Were they sincere or did they just use those promises to get elected? The teacher suggests that they set up a "Meet the Candidates Meeting." Half the group is to be an audience made up of the Hamelin townspeople, while the other half is to arrange themselves in chairs in the meeting room. After the room has been set up, the Candidates are to make short statements to the meeting, explaining why the people should vote for them.

To facilitate the meeting, the teacher asks that all the Candidates sit in a way which makes them feel that they are presenting themselves best to their audience. The audience is instructed to listen carefully so that, when all Candidates are finished, they may ask questions.

The Candidates Meeting begins. Some election promises from a Grade 7 group include:

If elected I promise:
• to bring down the price of real estate in Hamelin
• to make sure schools have enough teachers
• to make more parkland available for the children
• to keep the Mayor in line

99

- to keep inflation down
- to be an honest Councillor
- to try to get a youth representative on Council so that young people will have more of a say.

Sometimes a lively debate will ensue between audience and Candidates. Sometimes, however, they will just deliver their promises and there will be no debate. If the teacher wishes, she can then have the audience and Candidates change roles and repeat the process. The more the Candidates know about themselves, the more commitment there will be to the drama.

SETTING UP THE ROOM PHYSICALLY

The teacher and students discuss what a suitable arrangement would be for the Hamelin Council Chambers. Together they arrange the furniture in the room to represent the meeting room of the Town Council.

ESTABLISHING A SYMBOL FOR THE MEETING

Together the class and teacher make desk-size name tags from cardboard. These are placed on the table in front of each Councillor. Anything else which does not belong to the drama (pencil cases, toys, etc.) should be removed. Tell students that they are to think of the drama area as a theatre set. Therefore only those things that are vital to the drama belong there. The students can use their own names or invent names which they think are suitable for Hamelin Councillors. This will avoid the problem of some students using deliberately funny names which will interfere with the drama. If a student still makes up a funny name, just accept it as a serious effort. The other students take their lead from the teacher, and the drama proceeds.

STILL IMAGE

The teacher asks the students to pose for a photograph that will show the Councillors on the steps of the Town Hall, ready for a meeting one month after the children's disappearance. While they are frozen, the teacher narrates, "It is one month later in the town of Hamelin, a town which mourns for its children who have not been seen since they disappeared into the mountain. The people have dug into the mountain, and the army has searched the area many times, but no trace of the children or the Piper has been found."

THE MEETING

The teacher is in role as Mayor; the students are in role as Councillors.

The teacher says, "I am going to enter the meeting room now, in role as the Mayor, while you will enter in role as Councillors." She then collects a file folder containing all their letters and says, "Good morning, ladies and gentlemen. Let's get straight on with it, shall we?"

She enters the meeting room and sits down. The students follow.

The teacher, in role as Mayor, says, "There's certainly no need for an agenda. We all know what the purpose of the meeting is. (She produces the letters.) These are just a few of the letters which have been pouring into my office all month from the citizens of Hamelin, from the business community, and from parents. They are all upset. They all blame us for this terrible tragedy. Well, I want to tell you that I have been up all night. I have racked my brain to come up with a solution to this problem. I don't have one. Do you?"

The Mayor waits for a response.

A partial description of what ensued in a Grade 7 class follows:

S1: I think we ought to dig deeper into the mountain.

S2: Me too. I'm not satisfied that they aren't in there.

T: Of course we can do that. However, the army has been very thorough. They assure us that there is just no trace of the children.

S3: We could try.

T: We've been trying. Surely when the army tells us they aren't there, we have to believe them. They're experienced in searches like this.

S4: Yeah. If you keep digging, the mountain might fall in and then if the kids are in there, they'll get buried.

T: Indeed. Then we'd be responsible for their deaths.

S1: We have to do something.

T: Yes, but what? (silence)

S5: We should advertise a reward.

T: A reward?

S5: Yes, for the Pied Piper and the children.

T: How do you mean?

S5: Send out word to all the towns around here. Say we will pay for information about where the Piper is.

S6: And the children.

S5: Yeah.

T: How will we do that?

S6: Send out town criers with the news.

T: I see.

S7: I think the Mayor should do something. This is all his fault.

T: Oh, I see, we are going to start blaming people, are we? I refuse to take the flack for this one. This is not my responsibility.

S7: Yes it is. You're the one who promised to pay the Piper one thousand dollars or guilders. If you'd paid him, this wouldn't have happened.

Comment: There is a general chorus of agreement from the group who are more than happy to shift the blame to the Mayor. They want the adult teacher to solve this one. It's tough. Naturally, the teacher, in role, is not going to let them shift the responsibility for the drama onto one character. They are the ones who are going to think this through, not the teacher.

T: How like you, Councillor Smithers, to try to blame me instead of taking responsibility. Don't you remember? We were all there. We all shook hands with the man. I saw you do that yourself. Remember?

S7: I didn't shake hands with him.

T: Well, you were there. Isn't it the same thing? And you were there when he asked for his money. If you're such a saint, why didn't you pay him?

S1: There's no point in blaming each other. That won't solve anything.

T: Thank you, Councillor. That's a very good point.

S1: I think we should work together to try and get those children back.

(General chorus of agreement)

S10: They might be dead.

Comment: As can be seen from the above transcript, this group

102

of Grade 7s have just begun to warm up to the subject. Their
actual meeting was 45 minutes long and was spirited and
intense. During this time, the teacher, in role, tries to be as
non-committal as possible. She deliberately withholds her
expertise from the students so that they are forced to wrestle
with the problem themselves. The teacher also behaves as
much as possible as the Mayor would. He may not have any
ideas to offer, but he is the Mayor, and he has enough ambi-
tion and political savvy not to let the Councillors shift the blame
to him or take over the meeting entirely.

Sometimes a group of Councillors may want the Mayor to
resign. Of course, this Mayor refuses. After all, he is not responsible entirely, and he keeps reminding them of the meeting's
purpose, which is to get the children back. To keep the matter urgent, the Mayor injects tension by announcing that members of the press are outside waiting for a report on what the
meeting has decided. Saying things like, ''Ladies and gentlemen, may I remind you, as we sit here arguing among ourselves, that the press is waiting outside for an announcement
from us. They want to know at the end of this meeting just
what we plan to do. May I also remind you that the people
of this town are angry and they are waiting for your decision.
Is anyone prepared to go out there and say, 'We have no plans'?
I certainly am not.'' Such tension helps the role drama work
in the same way that tension makes theatre work.

After a thorough discussion, this group decides that the only
way to solve the problem is to get the Pied Piper back to a meeting so they can talk with him. They also decide that they should
try every way possible to attract him since no one knows where
he is. They decide to do the following:

- send out town criers with the message that they want to speak
  with the Piper
- circulate posters to neighboring towns, advertising the fact that
  the Town Council of Hamelin wishes to speak with him. (The
  earlier suggestion to offer a reward is rejected on the grounds
  that offering a reward treats him as if he were a criminal, and
  since he is very powerful, the Council decides to treat him very
  carefully.)

Two committees are struck, one to compose cries and the other to design posters. The group agrees that the Mayor can announce to the press that they have decided to try to negotiate with the Piper. He cautions the group not to make their own statements to the press, gets agreement on this, and adjourns the meeting.

REFLECTING

Out of role, the teacher and students discuss the drama. The students express their frustration at trying to decide how they could get the Piper to speak with them as they know so little about him and how he will react. There is also further discussion about how much responsibility the Council should take for this problem. One student still feels the Mayor is the one to blame as he was the one who spoke with the Piper. This leads to a general discussion of whether or not bystanders who do nothing when a crime is being committed are guilty or innocent. It also leads to an interesting discussion about whether a handshake is binding.

While the teacher was in role as Mayor, she treated some of the Councillors quite harshly, as political opponents are wont to do. She would not have been true to her role if she had let Councillors try to blame her without retaliating strongly. It is important that, out of role, the teacher comments on this in some way so that the students affected are reassured that it was the role speaking and not the teacher.

Being able to be both in the drama, as a participant, and later out of it (and hence being able to talk about the people in the drama objectively) is one of the great strengths of this way of working. In role, participants can be involved in the issues emotionally; then later, out of role, they can regard the issues coolly and unemotionally. The teacher may reassure a student by saying something such as, "Well, the Mayor was certainly sarcastic to you, wasn't he? Mind you, I guess politicians are often pretty rude to each other, especially when they are being blamed for something. I thought your Councillor did a good job of standing up to the Mayor, didn't you? It's hard when the Mayor really has more power than a Councillor, I guess." Once when I said something like this to a boy with whom the Mayor had been very rude, he responded smilingly that yes, the Mayor had more power now, but not for long as his Councillor would win the next election!

Session four
WRITING TOWN CRIES AND DESIGNING POSTERS

Out of role, the teacher discusses with the students what the qualities of a good town cry, or announcement, should be. The students discuss style, audience, purpose, and content. They discover that posters and cries have things in common, such as:

- Both are relatively brief ways of communicating.
- Both rely a lot on presentation. The crier must be expressive and the poster must be well designed to catch people's attention.
- Both have the same audience in this case, and they share the same purpose.

One student offers that some people would look at a poster before they would listen to the words of the cry, and others would do the opposite.

Both committees set to work composing and designing. The students work in pairs and small groups. The posters are displayed and the town criers present their cries to the class.

Session five
PLANNING THE NEXT STAGE OF THE DRAMA (LARGE GROUP)

The teacher asks the students, "Do you think these town cries and posters would work? Would the Piper agree to meet with the Hamelin Council?"

Unanimously they decide yes. (If the group decides that they wouldn't work, the teacher would ask them for other suggestions. If the group was no longer interested in the Pied Piper, or was just willing to accept that the children had gone forever, then the drama would end.) This group was very interested in meeting with the Pied Piper, so the teacher continued the drama which now has a new focus: How do you get someone to meet with you when you don't even know who the person is, and how do you negotiate with him once he is found?

The teacher says, "Suppose the Piper is attracted by the town cries and posters and he sends word that he will meet just once with the Council, and then only for a maximum of 30 minutes. What should we do next?"

The students say that they should plan some strategies for

dealing with the Piper. The teacher agrees and asks the students if they would like the teacher to play the Piper. They are enthusiastic about this. This means that a new Mayor must be found. One of the boys offers to play this role. Not all groups want the teacher to play the Piper. If someone else elects to play him, that is fine. Remember that one of the underlying principles of this way of working is that students share the power. You must accept their decision and help the person who has elected this role to be successful both for himself and for the drama.

(See notes at the end of this chapter on how to prepare a student who has elected to take on a pivotal role in the drama.)

PLANNING IN SMALL GROUPS

The students divide into small groups to plan what they are going to say to the Piper and how they are going to approach him. They understand that they will have to report back to the large group. The teacher circulates among the groups, posing questions which help the students think more deeply. For example, a group of students plan to force the Piper into releasing the children by capturing him when he arrives at the meeting. The teacher asks, "Is it a good idea to try force with someone who seems to have special powers? If he could take the children away so easily, what else might he be capable of?"

At the end of their discussions, this class decides to:

- treat the Piper civilly so he will not feel threatened or get angry
- plead for their children, explaining to him that the town really needs the children back
- offer him 50,000 guilders and be willing to go up to 100,000.

As the teacher circulates, she gets a feeling that this class is confident that offering the Piper vast sums of money is the key. There is a feeling that the money was the issue and that they just have to offer the right sum. This information is very important if the teacher is to play the Piper, because it is up to her/him to inject the meeting with the theatrical elements of *tension* and *surprise*. Getting a feeling for what the students expect helps the teacher prepare her/his role while circulating. (An alternate strategy is to make a list of what the group knows and feels about the Pied Piper. This was described in chapter 4, page 81.)

The room is set up as before with the name tags and a spare chair for the Piper.

SHARING THE POWER

The students are asked, "Would you like to begin the drama at the point where the Piper comes in, or would you like to begin the meeting yourselves while the Piper waits outside until you send for him?"

Comment: This is what Dorothy Heathcote calls a 'branching question'. It gives the students the power to choose while limiting the possibilities so they will not be overwhelmed. It is very different from saying, "What will we do now?" The students are able to choose which way they want the drama to proceed without getting bogged down in hours of discussion.

This group chooses to start the drama as the Piper walks in.

STOP-FRAME TECHNIQUE

To focus the group, the teacher uses a stop-frame technique (see chapter 4, pages 82-83). Among the initial reactions to the Piper's entrance are:

This is our last chance.
I hope we can raise all that money.
Why does he dress so strangely?
He can't keep the children forever.
What does he want with them anyhow?
He's weird.

The Piper's thoughts are spoken, "I'll give these people half an hour of my time and that's all." He sits. The meeting begins.

THE MEETING WITH THE PIPER

The group sets out to bribe the Piper. They apologize, saying that they made a mistake, and that they have been able to find 50,000 guilders. They offer this to him. He refuses. They offer him more. He refuses. This is the only strategy they have for negotiation.

However, the Piper doesn't want the money. They appear nonplussed. They offer him increasingly larger amounts of guilders in exchange for the children. The Piper explains that it is a matter of honor. They have broken a verbal contract. He refuses to negotiate, saying, "Do you think that you can buy me? Don't you understand that not everyone has a price?"

The Councillors get angry with the Piper, accusing him of being heartless. "Don't you care about our town's unhappiness?" demands one Councillor.

"Not really," replies the Piper coolly.

"Well, we do," counters another.

"Really?" answers the Piper. "What a pity you don't care enough for your townspeople to be honest and honorable Councillors. If you really cared about people, you would treat them fairly and honor the contracts you make with them."

The Councillors accuse the Piper of being to blame for the town's problems.

He answers quietly, "You must think a little about that one for if you had kept your bargain, this would not have happened."

"But what of the children? Surely you cannot take this out on them. They must be very unhappy without us,'" insists a Councillor.

The Piper assures them that the children are safe and happy, for they have lost all memory of Hamelin and the life they had before going into the mountain. The Piper suggests, however, that they should be more worried about themselves, for they are without honor. On this note, he leaves.

WRITING IN ROLE

The teacher steps out of role and asks the students, who are still in role as Councillors, to write in their diaries that evening after the meeting. Some extracts from students' diary entries follow.

Dear Diary,
Today we had a meeting with the Piper. He is such a dumb fool. We offered him twice or three times the money we had promised. If you think about it, he is right. We had our chance and we fumbled it.

Dear Diary,

Today the Council had a meeting with the Pied Piper. He doesn't seem to understand our problem. He is, as it seems, a very stubborn man. We offered him over and over again very large sums of guilders or anything that he would like but as I said he is a stubborn man, so we got nowhere with him. We asked him to lead us to the children, but he said that they were in a land and had forgotten about us, their town, etc. Later, after more discussion, he left. I am feeling awful.

Dear Diary,

Today we (The Mayor, Council and I) had a meeting with the mysterious Pied Piper. I am quite upset as he refuses any sort of payment to get our children back. I am upset, mad and sad about what has happened. What the Piper said today at the meeting really made me think about how important it is to be truthful. I wish that the children would return soon, as I am depressed.

Dear Diary,

Today we had our meeting as planned. I am sad to admit that it was unsuccessful and we failed to find a way to regain our children. I am mad at myself, for I wish now, although it is too late, that I had been more stubborn and thought of a way because I truly loved my two children and feel a deep sadness because of their loss.

Comment: Clearly, the writing is reflective and personal. It is interesting how complex the sentence structure of some of the work is, revealing the students' total involvement with the issues. When students are involved in a topic the writing flows, and they often use complex structures to express their thoughts and feelings.

REFLECTING

The writing is shared and a discussion ensues. This group of students was amazed that the Piper could not be bought. There is also a lot of discussion about whether the Piper was magical, or whether people just believed he was. A student likens the Hamelin children to those young people who follow a cult leader to become members of a cult. Another suggests they are like 'groupies' who follow rock musicians.

The students are also amazed that they didn't get a second chance. They discuss how often there isn't a second chance in life, but they always get one in school. The teacher points out that there are many times in history when children are separated from their homes, as in times of war. The teacher tells them the theories behind the Pied Piper and these are discussed. The students say that they would be able to negotiate with him better next time if there were one, and agree that although the townspeople lost this time, they learned a lot which would help them in future.

Playing an uncompromising role

Although this particular group of students did not persuade the Piper to release their children, this does not always happen. Many times the townspeople are successful in winning back their children. The key is this: As teacher, I want the students to win, but I will not just *let* them win. I will not make it easy for them since winning anything important in life is seldom easy. In role as the Piper, I first take a stance which surprises them. Because this group thought that money was the key to negotiating with me, I deliberately took a moral stance which this group was not prepared for and therefore not able to handle. They had not thought deeply enough about how they should negotiate with the Piper.

I recall meeting with another group of students who also tried to buy off the Piper. Then, too, I took a moral stand, lecturing about honor and how corrupt they were, and as the Piper turned to leave, a boy who had been silent said very firmly, "Just a minute, I want to say something to you." Of course I stopped and listened while this young man literally took the Piper to task. He pointed out that he had sat listening to the Piper lecture about morals and was sickened. What gave the Piper the right to be so high and mighty, he wanted to know? When he called the Councillors immoral, whose criteria was he using? The student went on to tell the Piper very firmly that, yes, the Councillors had been wrong. It was not right to break a contract and they should have honored it. However, worse than that in his mind was the immoral act of kidnapping, which was what the Piper was guilty of. He ended by saying to the Piper, "You, sir, are nothing more than a common kidnapper!"

Of course, in role as Piper, I was stopped in my tracks and the teacher part of me was cheering. I was so pleased with his wonderfully articulated argument. The part of me that was the Piper really did not know what to do, so I said, "You've given me a lot to think about." (True!) "I will go and think and meet with you again."

One of the Councillors asked, "How do we know you'll come back?"

"Because," answered the Piper, "you have my word." I then left.

Out of role, the discussion was very lively. I asked the students, "Do you think the speech made by this Councillor would convince the Piper?" They were unanimously sure that it would. This group had won and was feeling triumphant.

Interestingly, this could be the end of the drama if they are sure the children would be returned. However, this group, when asked what they wanted to do next, elected to go into role as the children in the other land. They wanted to experience the drama from another point of view. They also instinctively knew that if they got to a completely satisfactory ending, then the drama would be over. They were enjoying it too much for that and by taking it from another point of view we were able to prolong it another two weeks. They had discovered for themselves a valuable drama rule — *slow down the work*. If one rushes to happy endings, there is no journey. It is the journey which creates the thinking moments and the satisfaction. Usually it is the teacher who must find ways to slow down the work, while the students want to rush onward.

This was an exceptional group and a joy to work with. However, I have had many an impassioned plea from even quite young children who have convinced the Piper that the children should be returned. In role as Piper, I simply take the stance that I have the children and have no real reason to return them unless someone convinces me, *really* convinces me. I won't give them up easily, and students seem to enjoy that challenge.

I remember a plea by a Grade 5 boy in a class in East Vancouver, who suddenly found his voice and delivered an impassioned plea for the children, saying that he was appalled by the Councillors' talk of money when the children were still missing. He spoke more articulately on how much the life of one child was worth to society and how millions of dollars could never make up for the loss of one child who could grow up to be the hope of the town. He was sincere and passionate and convincing. The Piper was not expecting such eloquence from this boy, so again he retired to think about it (a good ploy when one is rendered speechless in role). Again, the students knew that the speech was convincing and were happy just to write their own ending, which was that the Piper was moved by this eloquence and the children were returned. End of a very satisfactory drama for this group.

Only the ground work of a role drama can be planned. After the plan is employed (in this drama the plan ended during the first meeting when the Mayor asks the Councillors what should be done), the teacher has to listen very carefully and be always looking for new learning possibilities. As the drama proceeds, many of these learning doors appear. The teacher's skill lies in thinking quickly which doors should be opened and entered and which should be left shut. Each door presents a different focus. Of course, if two appear simultaneously and the teacher is uncertain, the class can make the decision or at least help with it.

Writing possibilities

In this role drama, the students wrote business letters, personal diaries, and town cries. However, many other writing activities could be implemented. These include:

- Writing a biography in role. This could have been done before or after the students had created the mural of the Town of Hamelin.
- Writing newspaper headlines and articles about the rat problem, and then about the mysterious disappearance of the children.
- Writing an ending to the story.
- Writing an account of the events in the form of a story told by a grandmother, speaking to her grandchildren, 30 years after the event.

- Writing a description of the Town of Hamelin to go with the mural, for the town's museum.
- Writing in role as the Piper — perhaps a diary entry written after his meeting with the Councillors and Mayor.
- Writing a description of the Pied Piper.

Could a student play the role of the Pied Piper?

While it is perfectly acceptable for a student to take on the role of the Pied Piper, remember that the teacher must still be in the drama. Even if someone else insists on being the Mayor, the teacher must retain a strong presence in role — perhaps as a Councillor. This type of drama work differs from others in that the teacher always has a role within the drama. From within the drama, the teacher can shape the drama, pose the questions which make the students think, play devil's advocate, and open up new possibilities which challenge.

If a student wants to play the Piper, ask, "Are you able to take on this role seriously? Are you willing to try hard to think like this Piper and figure out things about him? I need to know this from you because it is an important role, and we all want assurance from you that you can do it. Can you? Indicate by the tone of your voice and your seriousness that this is very, very important. Give the student time to think about it. If the person is uncertain, say something like, "It's okay if you change your mind, but if you still want to do it and think that you can do justice to the role, I'll help you. What do you think?" If he still wants to do it, then he has had time to consider the commitment seriously, a major first step. Then set the class to work in groups to devise their strategies for the Piper, and take the Piper to a corner of the room and ask questions which will help him think more deeply about his role. For example:

Why do you want those children anyway?

Why have you come to the meeting?

Where do you live?

Where are the children?

How much are you willing to tell these Councillors?

Are you really magical or do you just know more than these people?

What does music mean to you?

Then both of you circulate, listening to the perceptions of the students and their plans for dealing with the Piper. Help the Piper plan an attitude which will surprise the group. If necessary, rehearse the beginning of the meeting together, and then let him be the Piper. The beauty of the teacher still being in the drama is that in role as a Councillor s/he can still ask the provoking questions or make challenging statements. The teacher can still work from within the drama to make this a learning experience.

Selected references

The Pied Piper. Retold by Manuela Lazzara Pittoni and Ester Piazza. Illustrated by Roberto Molino. Translated by Erica Propper. London: Macdonald Educational Ltd. (First published by Editrice La Sorgente, Milan, 1974.) Also contains Robert Browning's original story in prose.

The Pied Piper of Hamelin. Retold by Catherine Storr and illustrated by Anna Dzierzek. London: Belitha Press Limited/Milwawkee, Wisconsin: Raintree Publishers Inc., 1984. Includes many details of Browning's story; 32 pages, all double-page spreads; fascinating illustrations.

The Pied Piper of Hamelin. Retold and illustrated by Peter Weevers. London: Hutchison Children's Books, 1991. A rhythmic prose retelling with watercolor illustrations.

6

Evaluation

Many teachers who wish to use drama in education as a method of integrating learning in their classrooms are often unsure of how they should approach the problem of evaluating their students' work. These concerns are widely shared by educators and are concisely summarized by Morgan and Saxton (1987, 188) when they write:

> No systematic approach to evaluation in drama has evolved because the subject itself operates in a curriculum model which is heuristic (the pupil is trained to find out things for himself) rather than technological (the student is trained to assimilate a defined body of knowledge).

Evaluation in the drama learning process

The whole issue of evaluation becomes even more confusing if drama is used exclusively by the classroom teacher as a method of teaching another subject area, such as social studies, in a subject-oriented curriculum, or a theme or topic in an integrated curriculum. Whatever the purpose for using drama in the classroom, two basic principles should be observed: drama evaluation is qualitative in nature and plays a central role in the students' ongoing, overall learning process. In other words, evaluation should be seen as providing a means of fostering children's intellectual, emotional, and social development through their *active*, *creative*, and *reflective* engagement in the drama learning process.

Although differences of opinion have been expressed by many educators regarding the teacher's role in the ongoing learning process, there appears to be common consent that the teacher has a crucial role to play in structuring the dramatic experience, and providing continuous feedback to the students on their achievement and progress. One writer (Stabler 1978) describes drama evaluation as a cooperative venture between student and teacher, and stresses the importance of qualitative, ongoing evaluation.

Unfortunately, there is not a long tradition of research in the use of drama as a learning medium. Therefore little is known about the actual learning that occurs in drama in education, although writers from many other branches of learning have consistently attested to its beneficial effects, particularly in the areas of cooperative learning, the developing use and awareness of language, problem-solving, and the development of higher level thinking. In addition, there appears to be little data about the effects of different teaching approaches on student learning.

In spite of this lack of specific information about the effects of using drama in the classroom on student learning, drama curricula from different countries (including Australia, Canada, the United Kingdom, and the United States) share many common features with respect to the teaching and evaluation of drama in education. All curricula advocate a child-centred approach to the teaching of drama which values process over product, of 'the doing' and 'the making' over 'the performing'. Ways in which to evaluate student learning reflect this philosophy by explicitly or implicitly stating that evaluation of student learning should provide positive feedback to the student and remain as an integral part of the ongoing learning process.

As the Australian drama educator, John McLeod (1989) points out, the challenge for teachers of drama is to go beyond identifying *what* is learned in drama. McLeod (1985) says that one of the great myths about evaluation is that to be fair, consistent, transferable from one context to another, and accountable, the evaluation must be objective. However, whether teachers use a qualitative or a quantitative approach, which ultimately requires them to make judgments, the evaluation will inevitably be *subjective* and will greatly depend on the relationship of the evaluator to the student.

With this in mind, there are a number of precautions that any teacher wishing to evaluate students' work in drama should observe. First, the success of the dramatic action that is created in the classroom will largely depend on what the children bring to the experience and the ways in which they and their peers, in cooperation with the teacher, give shape and meaning to that experience. Therefore in creating a context in which children feel free to take risks by either expressing their feelings or taking a role, a set of formal, objective evaluation procedures or list of skills to be taught and assessed may threaten the climate of trust that the teacher is trying to establish.

In addition, students who do not contribute verbally to a drama may be intensely absorbed in the work. Outward appearances can be very deceiving, and the child who is the most outgoing participant in a drama may actually be deriving less from the experience than one who appears more shy and reserved. As the authors of *Drama in the Formative Years* (Ontario Ministry of Education, 1984) remark:

> In drama in education, one is attempting to assess the nature of an internal and personal process — of an inner experience — as well as to judge the external and public form.

Above all, drama is a shared experience in which it is impossible to separate the participants (students and teacher) from the dramatic context which they have created. Any assessment of learning in the drama classroom should not ignore this reality.

Determining what is to be evaluated

Although it is difficult to generalize for every teaching and learning situation *what* is to be evaluated in classrooms where drama is being used, four general areas based on those originally suggested by Cook (1979) might be considered as a starting basis for student evaluation. However, these areas should not be viewed as being mutually exclusive, as each area may be present in any drama work undertaken by a class. The four areas include:
1. The actual learning that is occurring (at an intellectual level and at an emotional level)

2. An understanding and appreciation of drama as an art form
3. The development of expressive and communication skills
4. Personal and social skills.

In all four areas the teacher is concerned with assessing student learning at both the individual and the group level. As has been noted, evaluating the *ways* in which students learn in drama is equally important as evaluating *what* is being learned. Because drama is a social art form, any change of understanding that might occur in the course of the drama experience cannot be viewed solely in terms of the individual alone but must also be assessed in terms of the group as a whole. Inevitably, this will influence not only the area of learning that is being emphasized in the evaluation but also the actual type of evaluation instrument the teacher uses.

For example, on some occasions the teacher might be concerned with evaluating a student's ability to reflect at a personal level on a situation that has occurred in the drama by writing thoughts in role (e.g., writing a journal entry about the meeting with the Pied Piper). Here the focus for evaluation is on learning area one, learning at the intellectual and emotional level. At another point in the same drama, the teacher may wish to assess how well the class is working together in a joint project by observing how they prepare the Council Chamber for the meeting between the Mayor and Council (area four, social skills). On yet another occasion, the class might work in small groups to create tableaux which show ways in which the people of the Town of Hamelin communicate to the Piper that they wish to meet with him (area four, understanding and appreciating the dramatic art form).

In each case, the area(s) of learning that are being emphasized are different as well as the actual type of evaluation procedure. In addition, there is a shift from individual evaluation to whole-class evaluation and finally to small-group evaluation. While the role writing activity offers each student the opportunity to respond to the drama at an intellectual and emotional level and to communicate thoughts and feelings as an individual, the small-group activity requires the students to work together to shape their ideas and understandings into dramatic form.

Although the focus of evaluation and the instrument may differ, all four areas of learning are likely being employed in each of these activities. For example, when the students are setting up the Council Chamber, the teacher may be observing their social skills in working together, but the students will also be required to plan and make choices and decisions (area one), use their knowledge and understanding of space in a theatrical sense (area two), and communicate with one another (area three).

Unlike other subject areas, in drama the teacher is in a unique position to observe students from the vantage point of teacher in role. By working in role with the students, the teacher is able to work alongside them in the drama, observing them and talking with them and thereby assessing their understandings of the work. In addition, the teacher can initiate periods of reflection outside the dramatic context in which the teacher and students can discuss issues raised in the drama. Self-reflection should enable students to assess their own change of attitude and understanding as a result of engaging in the drama.

Strategies used by students

Negotiations between students and between student(s) and teacher both within the dramatic context and during the reflective discussion periods outside the drama can provide a valuable source of information to the teacher about student learning in all four areas. From observations of junior secondary students negotiating both within and outside the dramatic context, Woody (1988, 18-19) compiled the following list of strategies used spontaneously by the students:

- anticipating and preparing for events
- signalling intentions, reading and responding to the signals of each other
- challenging each other, offering alternatives for decision-making, questioning assumptions and casting doubt
- changing direction, trying alternatives, giving new slants, testing ideas
- reassessing approaches, avoiding overused 'stale' methods, finding more suitable ways of dealing with content
- using tension, slowing the pace, using rituals and symbols and using space, light, sound, and silence levels imaginatively and deliberately
- seeing new implications in the work and deliberately deepening the level by stopping to reflect on the action.

This list of observations is particularly useful because it focuses on what the students can do and are accomplishing in their work rather than what the teacher thinks they should be doing. Drama curricula are filled with checklists of student behaviors, detailing what students should be accomplishing in their work as opposed to describing what students are actually doing. Thus, while the teacher may be looking exclusively for behaviors which appear to correspond with those on the checklist, often more critical and perhaps less obvious signs of student thinking and understanding are ignored.

Teacher strategies

Rather than adopt a preset and preconceived list of behaviors that the teacher determines a class of students should exhibit as a result of engaging in a dramatic activity, a more heuristic approach should be adopted in sympathy with the student-centred nature of drama itself. This does not mean that teachers cannot establish learning objectives for a drama activity and evaluate intended outcomes of the learning that have occurred both during and at the culmination of the activity. However, opportunities should be created that offer the widest possible means of evaluating student work in order that the teacher might be alerted to those student learning outcomes that may not have been originally planned for.

The sorts of opportunities most frequently used by teachers of drama which are integrated with the actual dramatic context in which the class is working include the following:

- responding to personal journals in which students record their reactions and reflections on the drama
- responding to students' writing in role during or after the drama
- responding to students' drawings, sketch work, and other artwork undertaken during the drama
- making individual, small-group and large-group observations and keeping anecdotal notes of student achievement and progress
- allowing time for reflective discussion both within and outside the dramatic context
- conducting individual and group conferences
- responding to group drama projects.

In each of these methods of evaluation, the teacher is reacting and responding to student work. At the same time, students themselves should be encouraged to respond to the drama work at a personal level and, if possible, react to the teacher's comment on their work. Creating an open climate of evaluation provides valuable information about the learning that is occurring in the classroom. It also provides feedback to the teacher about the relationship of the teaching to the student learning that has occurred, as well as to overall classroom organization and appropriate use of resources.

Students should be encouraged through their journal entries, in class discussions and individual conferences to comment on their growth in understanding about a drama theme or in one of the four areas of learning. Thus in a drama where the overall theme has been "Conflict with Authority", students are asked to make specific comments about any insights they have gained about the theme both during and after the drama. For example, the teacher might ask the students to relate the theme to a specific incident in their own lives or to suggest examples of the theme which may not have been included in the drama and could form the basis of further drama work.

General assessment questions

In a pilot curriculum drama project published in 1988 by the New South Wales Department of Education (Australia), the evaluation section included a number of useful general questions for teachers to ask themselves regarding their students' achievement in drama as well as about their own teaching methodology during a drama class. Here are some of the questions reclassified under the four areas of learning identified in this chapter:

INTELLECTUAL AND EMOTIONAL LEARNING

- Were the students able to use imagination to solve problems and understand issues?
- Did the students explore and develop their own feelings, attitudes, and values in a drama framework?
- Did the students explore and develop an understanding of other's feelings, attitudes, and values in a drama framework?

- Have the students developed an understanding of the need to imagine, accept and believe in a fictional context?
- Were the students able to take on and use role?
- Have the students developed an understanding of the ways in which role, tension, symbolization, and other theatre elements can be combined in a variety of forms?

EXPRESSIVE AND COMMUNICATION

- What skills in listening, speaking, reading, and writing have the students acquired and developed during their work in drama?
- To what extent are students becoming increasingly aware of the power of communication?

SOCIAL DEVELOPMENT

- Were the students able to work confidently, cooperatively, and effectively in a wide range of different grouping situations (e.g., pairs, small groups, and whole class)?

With regard to the teaching, the curriculum guide suggests the teacher uses the responses and reactions of the students to consider the following questions:

- Was the purpose of the drama activities made clear to the class?
- How effectively were different types of questions used to help the students structure their work and belief in the drama?
- How clearly were communications directed to the class?
- Were the activities relevant to the students' level of dramatic experience?
- Were the activities appropriately sequenced for conceptual development?
- Was the content of the drama activities appropriate to the needs, interests, and abilities of the students?
- Were activities varied across whole-class, small-group, and individual approaches?

Clearly both teaching and learning are closely integrated in drama, and any evaluation of and by students working in drama must play a central role in developing future drama learning experiences. Evaluation procedures which ignore this interrelationship may well transform drama in the classroom from a child-centred learning process into one that is solely dominated by the teacher's ideas and expectations for the students.

Selected references

Cook, Pat. "Evaluating Drama." *2D Journal*, 2, 1 (1979): 37-45.

McCleod, John. *Evaluating Drama*. Hobart, Tasmania: National Education Association for Drama in Education, 1985.

Morgan, Norah, and Juliana Saxton. *Teaching Drama: A Mind of Many Wonders*. London: Hutchinson, 1987.

New South Wales Department of Education. *Drama Syllabus K-6*. Sidney: NSW Department of Education, 1988.

Stabler, Tom. *Drama in the Primary Schools*. London: Heinemann, 1978.

Woody, Lynne. "Responsibility Learning and the Drama Process." *2D Journal*, 7, 2 (1988): 16-28.

Annotated bibliography

Children's books, stories, and poems offer a wide variety of possibilities for working in role drama. The following annotated bibliography gives further suggestions of ways in which you can explore story, language, and thinking through drama.

Barton, Bob. *Tell Me Another*. Markham, Ontario: Pembroke Publishers Limited/Portsmouth, New Hampshire: Heinemann Educational Books, 1986.
Bob Barton covers all the essential aspects of storytelling in a clear, concise, and eminently useful manner. From the simple beginning and progressing through the complete spectrum of types and forms of stories, *Tell Me Another* is filled with valuable activities and sage advice. Spiced with anecdotes from Bob's vast experience, this book is a must for teachers interested in storytelling in the classroom.
(elementary and intermediate)

Booth, David. *Games for Everyone*. Markham, Ontario: Pembroke Publishers Limited, 1986.
More than 100 games and activities are grouped around such general areas of learning as cooperating, building groups, problem-solving, movement, communication, and sense explorations. A short bibliography follows each grouping. On each page, a game is named, goals listed, and a clear, concise description of the game is provided, followed by useful extensions.
(elementary and intermediate)

Booth, David. "'Imaginary Gardens with Real Toads': Reading and Drama in Education." In *Theory into Practice* XXIV, 5, 1985: 193-198.
The author, a master teacher, has pioneered many drama teaching strategies in his exploration of the relationship between drama and reading. This article gives an overview of the under-

lying principles of his work, along with some useful practical examples of working with drama and story.
(elementary)

Booth, David, and Charles Lundy. *Improvisation: Learning Through Drama*. Don Mills, Ontario: Harcourt Brace Jovanovich, Canada, 1985.
Intended for secondary school students working in drama, the book is an excellent source of games and exercises for intermediate grades. It includes a full-length picture book, *The Expedition*, with suggestions on how to develop a drama based on the themes of the book.
(intermediate and secondary)

Byron, Ken. *Drama in the English Classroom*. London: Methuen, 1986.
Although this book is written with secondary teachers in mind, any teacher wishing to use drama to promote language and thinking will find this well-written description and analysis of a teacher's first attempts at drama work both illuminating and rewarding. The book is full of practical suggestions for illustrating literary themes through the use of drama.
(intermediate and secondary)

Davies, Geoff. *Practical Primary Drama*. London/Portsmouth, New Hampshire: Heinemann Educational Books, 1983.
Probably the most readable book on the subject of using role and story in the classroom, this book is crammed with practical tips for teachers of all grades, although Geoff Davies' anecdotes are from his primary teaching experience. It is a first-rate, practical introduction based on the author's first-hand teaching experience.
(primary and intermediate)

Neelands, Jonothan. *Making Sense of Drama*. London/Portsmouth, New Hampshire: Heinemann Educational Books, 1984.
This book is concerned with planning and negotiating in drama. Neelands draws on his own drama teaching experience to provide teachers with ideas for planning their own dramas. The book contains some excellent examples of dramas based on literature. However, it is not a beginner's book. Read it after you have worked your way through this one!
(intermediate)

Neelands, Jonothan. *Structuring Drama Work*. New York: Cambridge University Press, 1990.

In his latest book, Neelands refers to some 20 dramatic strategies — teacher-in-role, writing in role, role on the wall (outline of body), imaging, tableau, etc. but doesn't dwell at length on sources.

(all grades)

O'Neill, Cecily; Alan Lambert; Rosemary Linnell; and Janet Warr-Wood. *Drama Guidelines*. London: Heinemann Educational Books, 1977.

One of the classics about teaching drama across the curriculum. In addition to the clear, concise theoretical statements about many different aspects of drama in education, this book contains detailed descriptions of drama lessons taught from Kindergarten to Grade 12, a number of useful games, and teacher notes.

(all grades)

O'Neill, Cecily, and Alan Lambert. *Drama Structures: A Practical Handbook for Teachers*. London: Hutchinson/Portsmouth, New Hampshire: Heinemann Educational Books, 1982.

Filled with descriptions of dramas based on literary and social studies themes, and penetrating, perceptive reflections on teacher planning, alternative teaching strategies, and questioning techniques. Although this book is written for the intermediate and secondary teacher, it should be read by any teacher wishing to use drama in the classroom.

(intermediate and secondary)

Swartz, Larry. *Dramathemes: A Practical Guide for Teaching Drama*. Markham, Ontario: Pembroke Publishers Limited/ Portsmouth, New Hampshire: Heinemann Educational Books, 1988.

A first-rate introductory handbook for teachers wishing to use drama to enrich their language arts programs. Themes have been selected from across a wide range of literary genres, and the lessons are practical and easy to follow.

(primary and intermediate)

Tarlington, Carole, and Patrick Verriour. *Offstage: Elementary Education Through Drama*. Toronto: Oxford University Press, 1983.

A practical lesson-by-lesson approach to the teaching of drama

in elementary grades. It contains a wide range of games and drama exercises designed to enhance learning in the elementary classroom. Lesson descriptions are given for doing role dramas based on literary and social studies themes. The book also contains suggestions for performance drama.
(primary and intermediate)

* * * * *

In this book we have emphasized practical approaches because teachers want practical advice on how to do this work in their classrooms. However, it is also important to understand the theory behind this way of working, especially since it ties in so well with what we now know about the importance of whole language approaches to learning.

The last 15 years have seen a growth in research and writing about drama, its implications for the curriculum in general and language and thinking in particular. The following books are excellent guides to the theory and practice of drama in education.

Bolton, Gavin. *Toward a Theory of Drama in Education*. London: Longmans, 1979.
Based on his extensive experience as a reflective, innovative drama teacher, Bolton examines the existing theory and practice of drama teaching and makes a powerful case for drama which challenges the students' thinking and provides students with a change of insight and understanding.

Bolton, Gavin. *Drama as Education. An Argument for Placing Drama at the Centre of the Curriculum*. London: Longmans, 1984.
In his second book, Bolton traces the history of drama in education with special reference to its use across the curriculum. Again Bolton stresses the importance of recognizing the central role that the elements of theatre play in educational drama. No drama teacher can afford to miss this book.

Cazden, Courtnay. *Classroom Discourse*. Cambridge: Cambridge University Press/Portsmouth, New Hampshire: Heinemann Educational Books, 1988.

Davis, David, and Chris Lawrence, eds. *Gavin Bolton: Selected Writings*. London: Longmans, 1986.

A comprehensive collection of almost 20 years of Bolton's writings provides insight into many different aspects of drama in education. These include drama as an art form, drama and emotion, and drama and classroom practice.

Johnson, Liz, and Cecily O'Neill, eds. *Dorothy Heathcote: Collected Writings on Education and Drama.* London: Hutchinson/Portsmouth, New Hampshire: Heinemann Educational Books, 1984.
By reading this collection, anyone unfamiliar with the name of Dorothy Heathcote will soon realize why she is recognized as one of the great teachers of our time. Noted for her work in changing the face of drama teaching, she has also much to say about the art of teaching and the school curriculum. This collection captures her metaphoric style of thinking and writing.

Morgan, Norah, and Juliana Saxton. *Teaching Drama: A Mind of Many Wonders.* London: Hutchinson/Portsmouth, New Hampshire: Heinemann Educational Books, 1987.
A clear, thoughtful, and practical account of the art of drama teaching. The authors have unraveled the complexities, discarded the jargon, and presented the teacher of drama with one of the most helpful resource guides and handbooks ever written on the topic.

Wagner, Betty Jane. *Dorothy Heathcote. Drama as a Learning Medium.* Washington, D.C.: National Educational Association, 1976.
When B.J. Wagner set out to write a study of Dorothy Heathcote's teaching, she probably never imagined the impact that this book would have on drama teaching. For years it was the guide to Heathcote's work and to the teaching of drama across the curriculum. It is essential reading for anyone wishing to understand modern innovations in drama in education.

Watkins, Brian. *Drama and Education.* London: Batsford, 1981.
The delight of this lucidly written book is that it provides a comprehensive survey of an enormous range of issues and topics of concern to anyone interested in teaching drama. It includes thoughtful chapters on the game of drama, drama and the multicultural classroom, and on analysis of the drama lesson, among many other subjects.